J. PAUL MITCHELL,
the editor of this volume,
is Assistant Professor of History
at Southern Methodist University.
A native of Wisconsin,
he received his B.A. from Knox College in 1959
and his Ph.D. from the University of Denver in 1966.
He has taught at Memphis State University
and at Pennsylvania State University.

CONTENTS

v

RIOTS INCLUDED

| PLACE | DATE | NUMBER KILLED | |
		BLACK	WHITE
New York City	July 13–16, 1863	(unknown)	1000–1500
Memphis	May 1–4, 1866	46	2
Atlanta	July 22–24, 1906	11	2
Springfield	August 14, 1908	2	4
East St. Louis	July 2, 1917	39	9
Houston	August 23, 1917	1	18
Washington	July 19–23, 1919	4	3
Chicago	July 27–August 6, 1919	23	15
Tulsa	May 31–June 1, 1921	26	10
Detroit	June 20–21, 1943	25	9
Harlem	August 1–2, 1943	5	0
Los Angeles	July 11–17, 1965	30	1 (4 other)
Tampa	June 10, 1967	2	0
Newark	July 13–17, 1967	21	2
Detroit	July 23–27, 1967	33	10
Memphis	March 28, 1968	2	0
Washington	April 5–8, 1968	7	1

RACE RIOTS
IN
BLACK AND WHITE

☞ **1** ☜

INTRODUCTION

Our nation is moving toward two societies, one black, one white—separate and unequal.

(Report of the National Advisory Commission
on Civil Disorders, *1968*)

The Negroes read daily of lynchings; the whites read of Negro rape stories.

(The Messenger, *1921*)

Race riots crush, violate, shatter; they leave behind anxiety and perplexity. How to explain something so alien to the American way of life? Surely sinister outside influences—carpetbaggers, Bolsheviks, the Ku Klux Klan, Axis fifth columnists, Communists, black power demagogues—must be at work stirring up the criminal element of the city slums. At least, this is the most common reaction, of which the frantic concern with Federal anti-riot laws fostered by a steady succession of "long, hot summers" in the 1960s is but the latest example.

But race riots are not so aberrant as to be totally out of place in the United States. Rather, they are highly visible eruptions of the violence that has been both tacit and explicit in American race relations. To be sure, violence has only been the most spectacular, not the sole, mode of interracial behavior. And social violence has not been confined to interracial outbursts, as is attested by patriot mobs before the American Revolution, farmers' uprisings, labor battles, frontier justice, and even gang wars. Finally, social brutality and riots are not the exclusive property of the United States. Yet the fact remains that interracial violence is an integral part of the American past; from the black point of view, lynching is as American as apple pie.

The historical pattern of interracial violence, fear, and distrust is the result of a caste system which bestows dominance on whites while relegating blacks to a subordinate position. This rigid social system

1

belies the promises of the United States, where class structure has been relatively fluid and the expectation of upward mobility has been enshrined. This system is therefore highly frustrating to the subordinate caste members, all the more because its distinction, color, is so visible and so permanent. Violence, then, has resulted from the fundamental clash between the aggressive determination of the white, who must employ force to maintain his position of social superiority over the unwilling black, and the upward struggle of the black, who seeks to escape his subservient status.

Violence was seldom far from the surface during the two and one-third centuries of slavery, for the system was based on the principle of physical coercion. The slaves, actually owned by their superiors and totally dependent on them, presented a stance of general acquiescence. Lacking effective orderly channels of expression, those who were unresigned resorted to violence. This form of redress suggested itself since physical chastisement was part of the scheme of incentives. Most commonly, slaves diverted their violent resistance toward substitute persons or objects, thereby avoiding a suicidal confrontation with the slaveowner or overseer. Still, they rose up, singly and in groups, just often enough to keep white masters in a perpetual state of fear. Consequently, whites accepted physical punishment as both a right and a duty; they used violence to still white and instill black terror. That their beatings were as often dutifully as sadistically administered made them no less painful and degrading. Debates over the nature and continued existence of slavery in the mid-nineteenth century exploded in belligerent rhetoric. When the institution was finally abolished, it ended in the context of a civil war.

Violent conflict has continued to characterize interracial behavior since the end of slavery. Lynching, beating, and bombing by whites have supplemented legal systems of restraint designed to maintain white supremacy. Even these legal systems of social control have exceeded the proper limits of the state's monopoly on the use of legitimate force; all too often, law enforcers have condoned and indulged in extraofficial forms of violence directed against the subordinate race. Blacks have continued to protest against their status, sometimes peacefully through attempts at self-improvement, sometimes peacefully through demonstrations against external impediments, and sometimes violently when peaceful conflict seemed fruitless. This pattern of black pressure and white resistance has been rather consistent during the past century. And out of the climate of mutual suspicion that has accompanied this pattern, both sides have developed philosophies which justify violence directed against any or all members of the other caste. Whites claim the right to use whatever means are necessary to maintain their version of social order, usually articulated in terms of the purity of white womanhood and the supremacy of whites in a white man's country. Blacks plead self-defense and the right to pursue their stated goals of freedom, equality, and dignity.

Urban race riots have been of three basic types: white riots, in which whites have massacred blacks and property destruction has been secondary to outright personal assaults; white-black riots, in which groups of one race have attacked individuals or smaller groups of the other in an atmosphere of interracial war; and the most recent type, the black riots, in which property has been the main target for destruction and looting, and blacks have been the participants. The physical outcome of all three types is the same: of the dead and injured more are black than white, and the black ghetto is destroyed. In the first type, the whites do the destroying and blacks are killed, beaten as often as shot, by white civilian mobs as well as by white law enforcers. In the white-black riot, both white and black destroy, beat, and kill, but law enforcers are far more likely to kill blacks than whites. In the third type, blacks do the destroying and are killed, chiefly shot, by law enforcement agents.

Race riots have tended to cluster in historical settings notable for rapid economic, social, and political change. At such times, the subordinate blacks have exerted their strongest pressures against existing societal arrangements; the dominant-whites have perceived in this a challenge to their ability and determination to maintain white supremacy, and have reacted accordingly. In the past hundred years, urbanization and war have accelerated change, thereby fostering the conditions conducive to violent outbursts.

Urbanization has done much more than simply engulf American cities with hordes of ill-prepared rural migrants. The process itself multiplies the points of interracial friction. Residential and occupational invasion and succession are constantly at work, and are constant sources of hostility. In the city, self-selection and forced segregation have mobilized black communities with vast potential for self-assertion, communities whose very separateness is at once awesome and frustrating to those both inside and out. The urban way of life, dominated by secondary and tertiary relationships, offers a setting of greater personal freedom and more impersonal targets for wrath by both black and white; at the same time, these characteristics force a greater reliance on external, formal devices of social control, thereby increasing opportunities for open conflict.

Most race riots have occurred during or shortly following the Civil War, World Wars I and II, and the Vietnam War. This is no coincidence. War, with its massive mobilization on the home front, has speeded up the pace of change. Booming war industries have created jobs at the same time that manpower has been drawn off into the armed forces, producing spectacular migrations to urban industrial centers and opening up new areas of employment for blacks. Resulting competition for jobs and housing has exacerbated racial tension. Engaging in wars beyond its own boundaries, and relatively safe from territorial invasion, the United States (as did the North during the Civil War) has fought to preserve, not the United States directly, but "freedom" and "democracy"; its wars have been crusades. It has been difficult for blacks to reconcile this propaganda rhetoric with the realities of unimproved freedom at home, especially when they have been called upon to risk their lives in the crusade. Whites on the other hand have been anxious lest blacks allow their military experience to give them exalted ideas of "social equality." Amid daily accounts of wholesale killing and destruction, domestic violence may not appear so awful.

Given the underlying social pattern of American race relations, the mutual acceptance of violence, and the dynamic nature of a society enveloped in urbanization, war, and economic and technological change, the potential for overt interracial strife has been ever-present and formidable. When particular local settings augment these general conditions, a minor incident may spark a major riot. A lynching or threatened lynching, a rape or alleged rape, a fist fight, an everyday arrest, a rumor—all have served. But the match is not so important; the powder keg is always there and it does not take much of a spark to ignite the explosion.

Whatever the type of riot, it grips the city in an atmosphere half-carnival and half-terror. When the explosion burns itself out under military occupation, communities look for villains and create blue-ribbon interracial peace committees to prevent recurrences. Although "responsible" elements deplore the riot, not all people deprecate these holocausts. Nor are they unmitigated disasters, at least not for the rioters, who seem in the short run to achieve some positive gains. That blacks leave town after a white riot and that whites listen to blacks after a black riot attests to the efficacy of terror. But there is also the aftermath of devastation and intensified antagonism.

The selections in this book have been collected from a variety of types of sources, local and national, official and informal, expert and man-in-the-street, spokesman and individual. They are arranged topically rather than chronologically because the main elements of race riots—their long-range and immediate causes, the behavior of mobs and individuals, the efforts to restore order, and popular reactions—have had much in common regardless of the particular year in which a disturbance has erupted. Thus blended together, the selections are intended to give a black and white picture of the historical context of interracial violence in America.

☞ 2 ☜

SLAVERY

Interracial violence was firmly rooted in slavery. This characteristic was not always conspicuous, as the long debates over the nature of the peculiar institution disclose. Historians, as well as slavery's contemporary defenders and opponents, have been able to find ample evidence that in practice slavery was both benevolent paternalism and cruel exploitation. See, for example, Ulrich B. Phillips, *American Negro Slavery* (New York: D. Appleton and Co., 1918), and *Life and Labor in the Old South* (Boston: Little, Brown and Company, 1929), for the clearest statement of the paternalistic interpretation; Kenneth M. Stampp, *The Peculiar Institution: Slavery in the Ante-bellum South* (New York: Alfred A. Knopf, 1956), presents the coercive view. Thus, slaveholders have been portrayed as kindly or vicious, governed by humane concern and even love for their wards, or by avarice, brutal passion, and even sadism. Similarly, slaves have been pictured as docile and carelessly happy, or as resentful and fiercely resisting; their conduct has been ascribed to laziness and malevolence, or to shrewdness and a passion for liberty. The seeker can find what he looks for; if he needs to justify the past or to project into it values which would give historical sanction to some present course of action, he will likely succeed.

But whatever particular examples come to light, they must not obscure the essential fact that American slavery was based on force. The system subordinated one group to another; since black subordination was neither voluntary nor temporary, force and fear were so basic that violence was seldom far from the surface. The dominant whites used threatened and overt violence very effectively to instill fear in the hearts of blacks, and to quiet the fears of whites. Slaves resorted to violence to protest their subordinate condition, to escape from it, and even to try to destroy the system itself. Their resistance, however expressed, kept whites terrified and imparted a desperate quality to white retaliation. At the same time, the overwhelming power of whites conferred an even more desperate quality on black violence.

This same overwhelming white power also caused blacks to divert much of their violence from its principal object. Slave insurrections were spectacular but noteworthy rather than common; indeed, they existed chiefly in the minds of fearful slaveholders, who were ready to believe the wildest rumors and acted upon the flimsiest "evidence" of "conspiracies." More common were occasional retaliatory outbursts by recalcitrant slaves against physical punishment. But perhaps the violent nature of slavery shows most clearly in other modes of violent slave behavior, illustrating the phenomenon of displaced hostility: breaking tools, maltreating livestock, arson, self-mutilation, and even self-destruction. For their part, whites displayed their violence most visibly in their paranoid fear of insurrection, the savage repression which attended discovery of a "conspiracy," and the episodes of cruel treatment ending in the wanton deaths of some slaves. Not all masters and overseers were brutal sadists, however; indeed, that they were not monsters, that Simon Legree may not have been typical, bespeaks the fundamentally violent character of slavery as a system. Abolitionists claimed that slavery brutalized the master and his entire society; the matter-of-fact acceptance of a little whipping may well verify this claim.

Finally, out of the slave experience a rhetoric of violence became commonplace. Abolitionist talk was inflammatory and slaveholder determination to resist was menacing. Neither seemed to believe that slavery could end peaceably, and it did not; for, whatever its origins, a bloody and bitter civil war provided the immediate context in which slavery was ended.

"But I Takes the Freedom"

[From B. A. Botkin, ed., *Lay My Burden Down; A Folk History of Slavery* (Chicago: The University of Chicago Press, 1945), pp. 120, 267. All selections from this book are reprinted by permission of the publisher.]

Ex-Slave Mary Reynolds

Slavery was the worst days was ever seed in the world. They was things past telling, but I got the scars on my old body to show to this day.

Ex-Slave Henry Banner

What I likes best, to be slave or free? Well, it's this way. In slavery I owns nothing and never owns nothing. In freedom I's own the home and raise the family. All that cause me worriment, and in slavery I has no worriment, but I takes the freedom.

The Slave Trade

Fear was a constant companion of master and crew aboard a slave ship. Outnumbered usually by upwards of twenty to one, with cargoes of African captives only recently enslaved, these slave traders resorted to cruel extremes—chains, leg irons, and virtual entombment in the hold—for the sake of security. Despite precautions, slaves occasionally were able to lash out at their captors and the ensuing battles were fierce. The following selections from slave-ship journals show the bitter violence which attended the precarious Middle Passage of slaves from Africa to the Western Hemisphere. [From Elizabeth Donnan, ed., *Documents Illustrative of the History of the Slave Trade to America,* 4 vols. (Washington, D.C.: Carnegie Institution of Washington, II, 266, and I, 456–57.]

To return to Jaque a Jaques; we met there the *Robert* of Bristol, Captain Harding, who sailed from Sierraleon before us, having purchased thirty Slaves, whereof Captain Tomba mentioned there was one; he gave us the following melancholly Story. That this Tomba, about a Week before, had combined with three or four of the stoutest of his Country-men to kill the Ship's Company, and attempt their Escapes, while they had a Shore to fly to, and had near effected it by means of a Woman-Slave, who being more at large, was to watch the proper Opportunity. She brought him word one night that there were no more than five white Men upon the Deck, and they asleep, bringing him a Hammer at the same time (all the Weapons that she could find) to execute the Treachery. He encouraged the Accomplices what he could, with the Prospect of Liberty, but could now at the Push, engage only one more and the Woman to follow him upon Deck. He found three Sailors sleeping on the Fore-castle, two of which he presently dispatched, with single strokes upon the Temples; the other rouzing with the Noise, his Companions seized; Tomba coming soon to their Assistance, and murdering him in the same manner. Going after to finish the work, they found very luckily for the rest of the Company, that these other two of the Watch were with the Confusion already made awake, and upon their Guard, and their Defence soon awaked the Master underneath them, who running up and finding his Men contending for their Lives, took a Hand-spike, the first thing he met with in the Surprize, and redoubling his Strokes home upon Tomba, laid him at length flat upon the Deck, securing them all in Irons.

The Reader may be curious to know their Punishment: Why, Captain Harding weighing the Stoutness and Worth of the two Slaves, did, as in other Countries they do by Rogues of Dignity, whip and scarify them only; while three other, Abettors, but not Actors, nor of Strength for it, he sentenced to cruel Deaths; making them first eat the Heart and Liver of one of them killed. The Woman he hoisted up by the Thumbs, whipp'd, and slashed her with Knives, before the other Slaves till she died.

                              *   *   *

On the first day of January [1701], Casseneuve's journal takes notice of their sailing out of Cabinde being very unwholesome: which gave an opportunity to the slaves aboard to revolt on the fifth, as follows.

About one in the afternoon, after dinner, we according to custom caused them, one by one, to go down between decks, to have each his pint of water; most of them were yet above deck, many of them provided with knives, which we had indiscreetly given them two or three days before, as not suspecting the least attempt of this nature from them; others had pieces of iron they had torn off our forecastle door, as having premeditated a revolt, and seeing all the ship's company, at best but weak and many quite sick, they had also broken off the shackles from several of their companions' feet, which served them, as well as billets they had provided themselves with, and all other things they could lay hands on, which they imagin'd might be of use for their enterprize. Thus arm'd, they fell in crouds and parcels on our men, upon the deck unawares, and stabb'd one of the stoutest of us all, who receiv'd fourteen or fifteen wounds of their knives, and so expir'd. Next they assaulted our boatswain, and cut one of his legs so round the bone, that he could not move, the nerves being cut through; others cut our cook's throat to the pipe, and others wounded three of the sailors, and threw one of them over-board in that condition, from the fore-castle into the sea; who, however by good providence, got hold of the bowlin of the fore-sail, and sav'd himself, along the lower wale of the quarter-deck, where, (says Casseneuve) we stood in arms, firing on the revolted slaves, of whom we kill'd some, and wounded many: which so terrify'd the rest, that they gave way, dispersing themselves some one way and some another between decks, and under the forecastle; and many of the most mutinous, leapt over board, and drown'd themselves in the ocean with much resolution, shewing no manner of concern for life. Thus we lost twenty-seven or twenty-eight slaves, either kill'd by us, or drown'd; and having master'd them, caused all to go betwixt decks, giving them good words. The next day we had them all again upon deck, where they unanimously declar'd, the Menbombe slaves had been the contrivers of the mutiny, and for an example we caused about thirty of the ringleaders to be severely whipt by all our men that were capable of doing that office.

Punishing Slaves

The system of incentives which activated slavery was in large part negative. If slaves worked hard often it was due to fear of reduction in rations, demotion to a field gang (if they were not already in one), and sale to a cruel master or "down the river." Fear of a few lashes "well-laid on" might also, it was hoped, induce them to labor more diligently than the permanence of their slave status inclined them. Even more importantly, physical punishment was basic to the system of social sanctions designed to maintain law and order. The slave who disobeyed instructions, broke house rules, absented himself without permission, or violated the code of etiquette by striking, talking back to, or even gazing insolently at a white person presented a threat to the existing social order which required immediate repression. Attitudes fostered by the master-slave relationship made it likely that masters would respond with physical chastisement. (Sixty years after Emancipation a respected historian could write that given the primitive state of the slaves' development, swift physical punishment was the best means of meting out justice. John Spencer Bassett, *The Southern Plantation Overseer, as Revealed in His Letters* [Northampton, Mass.: Smith College, 1925], pp. 15–16).

Ex-slave Allen V. Manning recalls an episode on the Mississippi plantation where he had lived. [From Botkin, *Lay My Burden Down,* pp. 95–96.]

About that time Mr. Sears come riding down the big road. He was a deacon in Old Master's church, and he see us all packed up to leave, and so he light at the big gate and walk up to where we is. He ask Old Master where we all lighting out for, and Old Master say for Louisiana. We Negroes don't know where that is. Then Old Deacon say what Old Master going to do with Andy, 'cause there stood Mr. Clements holding his bloodhounds and Old Master had his cat-o'-nine-tails in his hand.

Old Master say just watch him, and he tell Andy if he can make it to that big black-gum tree down at the gate before the hounds git him, he can stay right up in that tree and watch us all drive off. Then he tell Andy to git!

Poor Andy just git hold of the bottom limbs when the bloodhounds grab him and pull him down onto the ground. Time Old Master and Mr. Clements git down there, the hounds done tore off all Andy's clothes and bit him all over bad. He was rolling on the ground and holding his shirt up round his throat when Mr. Clements git there and pull the hounds off of him.

Then Old Master light in on him with that cat-o'-nine-tails, and I don't know how many lashes he give him, but he just bloody all over and done fainted pretty soon. Old Deacon Sears stand it as long as he can and then he step up and grab Old Master's arm and say, "Time to stop, Brother! I'm speaking in the name of Jesus!" Old Master quit then, but he still powerful mad. I don't think he believe Andy going to make that tree when he tell him that.

Then he turn on Andy's brother and give him a good beating too, and we all drive off and leave Andy setting on the ground under a tree and Old Deacon standing by him. I don't know what ever become of Andy, but I reckon maybe he went and live with Old Deacon Sears until he was free.

When I think and remember it, it all seems kind of strange, but it seem like Old Master and Old Deacon both think the same way. They kind of understand that Old Master had a right to beat his Negro all he wanted to for running off, and he had a right to set the hounds on him if he did. But he shouldn't of beat him so hard after he told him he was going to let him off if he made the tree, and he ought to keep his word even if Andy was his own slave. That's the way both them white men had been taught, and that was the way they both lived.

Ex-slave Katie Rowe recalls a tragedy on an Arkansas plantation. [From Botkin, *Lay My Burden Down*, pp. 106–7.]

Old Man Saunders was the hardest overseer of anybody. He would git mad and give a whipping sometime, and the slave wouldn't even know what it was about.

My Uncle Sandy was the lead row nigger, and he was a good nigger and never would touch a drap of liquor. One night some the niggers git hold of some liquor somehow, and they leave the jug half full on the step of Sandy's cabin. Next morning Old Man Saunders come out in the field so mad he was pale.

He just go to the lead row and tell Sandy to go with him and start toward the woods along Bois d'Arc Creek, with Sandy following behind. The overseer always carry a big heavy stick, but we didn't know he was so mad, and they just went off in the woods.

Pretty soon we hear Sandy hollering, and we know old overseer pouring it on, then the overseer come back by hisself and go on up to the house.

Come late evening he come and see what we done in the day's work, and go back to the quarters with us all. When he git to Mammy's cabin, where Grandmammy live too, he say to Grandmammy, "I sent Sandy down in the woods to hunt a hoss, he gwine come in hungry pretty soon. You better make him a extra hoecake," and he kind of laugh and go on to his house.

Just soon as he gone, we all tell Grandmammy we think he got a whipping, and sure 'nough he didn't come in.

The next day some white boys finds Uncle Sandy where that overseer done killed him and throwed him in a little pond, and they never done nothing to Old Man Saunders at all!

When he go to whip a nigger he make him strip to the waist, and he take a cat-o'-nine-tails and bring the blisters, and then bust the blisters with a wide strap of leather fastened to a stick handle. I seen the blood running outen many a back, all the way from the neck to the waist!

Many the time a nigger git blistered and cut up so that we have to git a sheet and grease it with lard and wrap 'em up in it, and they have to wear a greasy cloth wrapped around they body under the shirt for three-four days after they git a big whipping!

Ex-Slave Mother Anne Clark.

[From Botkin, *Lay My Burden Down*, p. 55.]

My papa was strong. He never had a licking in his life. He helped the master, but one day the master says, "Si, you got to have a whopping," and my poppa says, "I never had a whopping and you can't whop me." And the master says, "But I can kill you," and he shot my papa down. My momma took him in the cabin and put him on a pallet. He died.

[From Frederick Douglass, *Life and Times of Frederick Douglass Written by Himself* (Hartford: Park Publishing Co., 1881), pp. 82, 60, 64.]

While I heard of numerous murders committed by slaveholders on the Eastern Shore of Maryland, I never knew a solitary instance where a slaveholder was either hung or imprisoned for having murdered a slave. The usual pretext for such crimes was that the slave had offered resistance. Should a slave, when assaulted, but raise his hand in self-defense, the white assaulting party was fully justified by southern law and southern public opinion in shooting the slave down, and for this there was no redress.

*   *   *

In Mr. James Hopkins, the succeeding overseer, we had a different and better man, as good perhaps as any man could be in the position of a slave overseer. Though he sometimes wielded the lash, it was evident that he took no pleasure in it and did it with much reluctance.

*   *   *

When the horn was blown there was a rush for the door, for the hindermost one was sure to get a blow from the overseer.

"And, Child, You Should Have Seen How She Chopped This Man to a Bloody Death"

The old image of the happy slaves singing in the moonlight was based on the belief that slaves were contented with their lot; how else could one explain the institution's longevity? Even with the limited resources at the historians' disposal, it is possible to suggest that most slaves somehow managed to accept their fate without implying that they failed to protest. Indeed, it is probable that many slaves were able to come to terms with their bondage precisely because they resisted total subjugation: they found outlets for their hostility which allowed them to survive. Although whites enjoyed overwhelming power over them, slaves had readily at hand objects which they could substitute for their masters and overseers and which they could attack in relative safety. Thus slaves destroyed tools and capital goods, stole, were careless with fire, maltreated livestock, and ruined crops. Most tragically, they also turned their resentment inward, punishing their masters by destroying their most valuable property, themselves. While this diverted resentment may have been a charade it was a violent charade. Another, drastic, alternative was to run away; since severe punishment surely visited failure, flight and its prevention involved desperate violence. Finally, in exasperation, a slave occasionally threw caution to the winds and lashed out directly at his tormentor. [From F. L. Olmsted, *A Journey in the Seaboard States* (New York: Dix and Edwards, 1856), pp. 105, 47.]

In working niggers, we must always calculate that they will not labor at all except to avoid punishment, and they will never do more than just enough to save themselves from being punished, and no amount of punishment will prevent their working carelessly or indifferently. It always seems on the plantation as if they took pains to break all the tools and spoil all the cattle that they possibly can, even when they know they'll be directly punished for it.

❋   ❋   ❋

So, too, when I ask why mules are so universally substituted for horses on the farm, the first reason given, and confessedly the most conclusive one, is, that horses cannot bear the treatment they always *must* get from negroes; horses are always soon foundered or crippled by them, while mules will bear cudgeling, and lose a meal or two now and then, and not be materially injured, and they do not take cold or get sick if neglected or overworked. But I do not need to go further than to the window of the room in which I am writing, to see, at almost any time, treatment of cattle that would insure the immediate discharge of the driver, by almost any farmer owning them in the North.

[From C. G. Parsons, *Inside View of Slavery; Or a Tour Among the Planters* (Boston: J. P. Jewett and Company, 1855), p. 212.]

"Sylva says," Mrs. A continued, "that she had been the mother of thirteen children, every one of whom she destroyed with her own hands, in their infancy, rather than have them suffer in slavery!"

[From James Redpath, *The Roving Editor; or, Talks with Slaves in the Southern States* (New York, 1859), pp. 252–53.]

A young girl, of twenty years or thereabouts, was the next commodity put up. Her right hand was entirely useless—"dead," as she aptly called it. One finger had been cut off by a doctor, and the auctioneer stated that she herself chopped off the other finger—her forefinger—because it hurt her, and she thought that to cut it off would cure it.

"Didn't you cut your finger off" asked a man, "Kase you was mad?"

She looked at him quietly, but with a glance of contempt, and said:

"No, you see it was a sort o' sore, and I thought it would be better to cut it off than be plagued with it."

Several persons around me expressed the opinion that she had done it willfully, to spite her master or mistress, or to keep her from being sold down South.

Ex-Slave T. W. Cotton

[From Botkin, *Lay My Burden Down*, p. 184.]

She hung herself to keep from getting a whupping. Mother raised her boy. She told Mother she would kill herself before she would be whupped. I never heard what she was to be whupped for. She thought she would be whupped. She took a rope and tied it to a limb and to her neck and then jumped. Her toes barely touched the ground. They buried her in the cemetery on the old Ed Cotton place.

Ex-Slave Heywood Ford

[From Botkin, *Lay My Burden Down*, pp. 176–77.]

White folks, ... I's gonna tell you a story 'bout a mean overseer and what happened to him during the slavery days. It all commenced when a nigger named Jake Williams got a whupping for staying out after the time on his pass done give out. All the niggers on the place hated the overseer worse than pizen, 'cause he was so mean and used to try to think up things to whup us for.

One morning the slaves was lined up ready to eat their breakfast, and Jake Williams was a-petting his old red-bone hound. 'Bout that time the overseer come up and seed Jake a-petting his hound, and he say: "Nigger, you ain't got time to be a-fooling 'long that dog. Now make him git." Jake tried to make the dog go home, but the dog didn't want to leave Jake. Then the overseer pick up a rock and slam the dog in the back. The dog, he then went a-howling off.

That night Jake, he come to my cabin and he say to me: "Heywood, I is gonna run away to a free state. I ain't a-gonna put up with this treatment no longer. I can't stand much more." I gives him my hand, and I say: "Jake, I hopes you gits there. Maybe I'll see you again sometime."

"Heywood," he says, "I wish you'd look after my hound Belle. Feed her and keep her the best you can. She a mighty good possum and coon dog. I hates to part with her, but I knows that you is the best person I could leave her with." And with that Jake slip out the door, and I seed him a-walking toward the swamp down the long furrows of corn.

It didn't take that overseer long to find out that Jake done run away, and when he did, he got out the bloodhounds and started off after him. It wa'n't long afore Jake heard them hounds a-howling in the distance. Jake, he was too tired to go any further. He circled round and doubled on his tracks so as to confuse the hounds and then he clumb a tree. 'Twa'n't long afore he seed the light of the overseer coming through the woods, and the dogs was a-gitting closer and closer. Finally they smelled the tree that Jake was in, and they started barking round it. The overseer lift his lighted pine knot in the air so's he could see Jake. He say, "Nigger, come on down from there. You done wasted 'nough of our time." But Jake, he never move nor make a sound, and all the time the dogs kept a-howling and the overseer kept a-swearing. "Come on down," he say again. "Iffen you don't I's coming up and knock you outen the tree with a stick." Jake, still he never moved, and the overseer began to climb the tree. When he got where he could almost reach Jake, he swung that stick, and it come down on Jake's leg and hurt him terrible. Jake, he raised his foot and kicked the overseer right in the mouth, and that white man went a-tumbling to the ground. When he hit the earth, them hounds pounced on him. Jake, he then lowered hisself to the bottom limbs so's he could see what had happened. He saw the dogs a-tearing at the man and he holler: "Hold him, Belle! Hold him, gal!" The leader of that pack of hounds, white folks, wa'n't no bloodhound. She was a plain old red-bone possum and coon dog, and the rest done just like she done, tearing at the overseer's throat. All the while, Jake he a-hollering from the tree for the dogs to git him. 'Twa'n't long afore them dogs tore that man all to pieces. He died right under that maple tree that he run Jake up. Jake, he and that coon hound struck off through the woods. The rest of the pack come home.

[The following two selections are from, respectively, the Tennessee *Gazette & Mero District Advertiser* and the Louisiana *Journal,* in U. B. Phillips, *Plantation and Frontier, 1649–1863,* 2 vols., *A Documentary History of American Industrial Society* (Cleveland: The A. H. Clark Company, 1910), II, 87–88.]

Advertisement, Nashville, Tenn. (November 7, 1804)

STOP THE RUNAWAY. FIFTY DOLLARS REWARD.

. . . The above reward will be given any person that will take him and deliver him to me, or secure him in jail so that I can get him.

If taken out of the state, the above reward, and all reasonable expenses paid—and ten dollars extra for every hundred lashes any person will give him to the amount of three hundred.

ANDREW JACKSON, near Nashville, State of Tennessee.

Advertisement, St. Francisville, La.

RUNAWAY SLAVE. Is detained in the public prison of the Parish of Point Coupee, as a runaway, a negro about twenty years of age, calls himself William, he is Black and has a down look, five feet seven inches high, when committed, had around his neck an Iron collar with three prongs extending upwards, has many scars on his back and shoulders from the whip.

Ex-Slave John Henry Kemp

[From Botkin, *Lay My Burden Down,* p. 175.]

One day when an old woman was plowing in the field, an overseer came by and reprimanded her for being so slow—she gave him some back talk, he took out a long closely woven whip and lashed her severely. The woman became sore and took her hoe and chopped him right across his head, and, child, you should have seen how she chopped this man to a bloody death.

Nat Turner's Rebellion

Slave revolts were not as common as slaveholders' paranoia might have indicated; indeed, historical evidence for their occurence remains elusive, especially where the alleged revolt never passed the plotting stage. The perpetual fear of insurrection nearly amounted to a self-fulfilling expectation: whites were insecure, prepared to suppress an uprising, and needing to believe that slaves were always plotting in order to sanction existing systems of forceful restraint; consequently, they were receptive to rumors and ready to project conspiracies into even slightly suspicious actions. Extorted "confessions" complicate the historical record, which makes it clear that most "insurrections" were actually abortive and unconfirmed plots. Among the few noteworthy rebellions were the uprising in New York City in 1712, the Cato conspiracy in South Carolina in 1739, Gabriel Prosser's revolt in Richmond in 1800, and Nat Turner's Rebellion in Southampton,

Virginia in 1831. These revolts were bloody affairs, for slaves killed indiscriminately and whites first put them down with maximum force and then executed fair numbers. After the revolt in 1712 Governor Robert Hunter of New York wrote of the twenty-one slaves executed, "Some were burnt others hanged, one broke on the wheele, and one hung a live in chains in the town, so that there has been the most exemplary punishment inflicted that could possibly be thought of . . . " (E. B. O'Callaghan, ed., *Documents Relative to the Colonial History of the State of New York* [Albany: Weed, Parsons and Company, 1855] Vol. V, 341.)

Nat Turner was a slave who believed that divine powers had chosen him to lead his people out of slavery. Accordingly, he and a band of followers launched an uprising which struck terror in the hearts of whites throughout the South. In less than two days they murdered sixty whites and lost over 100 men in the fighting. Seventeen of the black survivors, including Turner, were executed. [From *The Confessions of Nat Turner, The Leader of the Late Insurrection in Southampton, Va., As fully and voluntarily made to Thomas R. Gray* (Baltimore: 1831); reprinted in *The Liberator,* December 17, 1831, pp. 202–3.]

I saluted them on coming up, and asked Will how came he there, he answered, his life was worth no more than others, and his liberty as dear to him. I asked him if he thought to obtain it? He said he would, or lose his life. This was enough to put him in full confidence. Jack, I knew, was only a tool in the hands of Hark. It was quickly agreed we should commence at home (Mr. J. Travis') on that night, and until we had armed and equipped ourselves, and gathered sufficient force, neither age nor sex was to be spared, (which was invariably adhered to). We remained at the feast, until about two hours in the night, when we went to the house and found Austin; they all went to the cider press and drank, except myself. On returning to the house, Hark went to the door with an axe, for the purpose of breaking it open, as we knew we were strong enough to murder the family, if they were awaked by the noise; but reflecting that it might create an alarm in the neighborhood, we determined to enter the house secretly, and murder them whilst sleeping. Hark got a ladder and set it against the chimney, on which I ascended, and hoisting a window, entered and came down the stairs, unbarred the door, and removed the guns from their places. It was then observed that I must spill the first blood. On which, armed with a hatchet, and accompanied by Will, I entered my master's chamber; it being dark, I could not give a death blow; the hatchet glanced from his head, he sprang from the bed and called his wife, it was his last word. Will laid him dead, with a blow of his axe, and Mrs. Travis shared the same fate, as she lay in bed. The murder of this family, five in number, was the work of

a moment, not one of them awoke; there was a little infant sleeping
in a cradle, that was forgotten, until we had left the house and gone
some distance, when Henry and Will returned and killed it; we got
here, four guns that would shoot, and several old muskets, with a
pound or two of powder. We remained some time at the barn, where
we paraded; I formed them in a line as soldiers, and after carrying
them through all the manoeuvres I was master of, marched them off
to Mr. Salathul Francis', about six hundred yards distant. Sam and
Will went to the door and knocked. Mr. Francis asked who was there?
Sam replied it was him, and he had a letter for him, on which he
got up and came to the door; they immediately seized him, and
dragging him out a little from the door; he was dispatched by repeated
blows on the head; there was no other white person in the family.
We started from there for Mrs. Reese's, maintaining the most perfect
silence on our march, where finding the door unlocked, we entered,
and murdered Mrs. Reese in her bed, while sleeping; her son awoke,
but it was only to sleep the sleep of death, he had only time to say
who is that, and he was no more. From Mrs. Reese's we went to Mrs.
Turner's, a mile distant, which we reached about sunrise, on Monday
morning. Henry, Austin, and Sam, went to the still, where, finding
Mr. Peebles, Austin shot him, and the rest of us went to the house;
as we approached, the family discovered us, and shut the door. Vain
hope! Will, with one stroke of his axe, opened it, and we entered and
found Mrs. Turner and Mrs. Newsome in the middle of a room, almost
frightened to death. Will immediately killed Mrs. Turner, with one
blow of his axe. I took Mrs. Newsome by the hand, and with the
sword I had when I was apprehended, I struck her several blows
over the head, but not being able to kill her, as the sword was dull.
Will turning around and discovering it, despatched her also. A general
destruction of property and search for money and ammunition, always
succeeded the murders. By this time my company amounted to fifteen,
and nine men mounted, who started for Mrs. Whitehead's (the other
six were to go through a by way to Mr. Bryant's and rejoin us at Mrs.
Whitehead's,) as we approached the house, we discovered Mr. Richard
Whitehead standing in the cotton patch, near the lane fence; we called
him over into the lane, and Will, the executioner, was near at hand,
with his fatal axe, to send him to an untimely grave. As we pushed
on to the house, I discovered some one run round the garden, and
thinking it was some of the white family, I pursued them, but finding
it was a servant girl belonging to the house, I returned to commence
the work of death, but they whom I left, had not been idle; all the
family were already murdered, but Mrs. Whitehead and her daughter
Margaret. As I came round to the door I saw Will pulling Mrs. Whitehead out of the house, and at the step he nearly severed her head

from her body, with his broad axe. Miss Margaret, when I discovered her, had concealed herself in the corner, formed by the projection of cellar cap from the house; on my approach she fled, but was soon overtaken, and after repeated blows with a sword, I killed her by a blow on the head, with a fence rail. By this time, the six who had gone by Mr. Bryant's, rejoined us, and informed me they had done the work of death assigned them. We again divided, part going to Mr. Richard Porter's, and from thence to Nathaniel Francis', the others to Mr. Howell Harris', and Mr. T. Doyles. On my reaching Mr. Porter's, he had escaped with his family. I understood there, that the alarm had already spread and I immediately returned to bring up those sent to Mr. Doyles, and Mr. Howell Harris'; the party I left going on the Mr. Francis', having told them I would join them in that neighborhood. I met these sent to Mr. Doyles and Mr. Harris' returning, having met Mr. Doyle on the road and killed him; and learning from some who joined them, that Mr. Harris was from home, I immediately pursued the course taken by the party gone on before; but knowing they would complete the work of death and pillage at Mr. Francis' before I could get there, I went to Mr. Peter Edwards', expecting to find them there, but they had been here also. I then went to Mr. John T. Barrow's, they had been here and murdered him. I pursued on their track to Capt. Newit Harris', where I found the greater part mounted and ready to start; the men now amounting to about forty, shouted and hurraed as I rode up, some were in the yard, loading their guns, others drinking. They said Captain Harris and his family had escaped, the property in the house they destroyed, robbing him of money and other valuables. I ordered them to mount and march instantly, this was about nine or ten o'clock, Monday morning. I proceeded to Mr. Levi Waller's, two or three miles distant. I took my station in the rear, and as it was my object to carry terror and devastation wherever we went, I placed fifteen or twenty of the best armed and most relied on, in front, who generally approached the houses as fast as their horses could run; this was for two purposes, to prevent escape and strike terror to the inhabitants—on this account I never got to the houses, after leaving Mr. Whitehead's, until the murders were committed, except in one case. I sometimes got in sight in time to see the work of death completed, viewed the mangled bodies as they lay, in silent satisfaction, and immediately started in quest of other victims.—Having murdered Mrs. Waller and ten children, we started for Mr. William Williams'—having killed him and two little boys that were there; while engaged in this, Mrs. Williams fled and got some distance from the house, but she was pursued, overtaken, and compelled to get up behind one of the company, who brought her back, and after showing her the mangled body of her lifeless husband, she was told to get down and lay by his side, where she was shot dead. I then started for Mr. Jacob Williams, where the family were murdered—Here we found a young man named Drury, who had come on business with Mr. Williams—he was pursued, overtaken and shot. Mrs. Vaughan was the next place we visited—and after murdering the family here, I determined on starting for Jerusalem.

After such an outburst, culprits must be found. Mrs. Lawrence Lewis, niece of George Washington, wrote to Mayor Harrison Gray Otis of Boston, on October 17, 1831. [From Samuel Eliot Morison, *The Life and Letters of Harrison Gray Otis, Federalist 1765–1848* (Boston: Houghton Mifflin Company, 1913), Vol. II, 259–60.]

Dear Sir,

I hope you will pardon my appeal to you, in consideration of our long acquaintance, & of the momentous & vital interests of which I am about to treat. The dreadful events of August last in our State, the want of confidence & insecurity produced by those horrors, *compel* me to address you. To a wretch outraging the Laws of God & Man, to the Editor of the "Liberator"—one of your community,—protected by your Laws, we owe in *greatest measure* this calamity. His paper is widely circulated even in this Town. Think you not that the blood of the innocent, the helpless, will be required of those who suffer such inflammatory publications to issue from their community, without the slightest check of *fine* or imprisonment. I think he merits *Death*—you would pronounce sentence of Death, on an Incendiary who would fire your City, throw a match into your powder magazine. Is not the Editor of the Liberator an incendiary of the very worst description—He inculcates insurrection, murder, cruelty, & baseness, in every shape. The most *lenient* are as frequently the victims, as the most rigorous, & even *more* frequently; since *nine* times out of *ten,* a negro loves those best who are *least* indulgent—*fear* not *principle* governing the *far far* greater part. Our whites unhappily evince *too much fear* of these wretches—they can *never* succeed in subjugating the Whites, but our young & lovely females, infant innocence, & helpless age will be their victims—it is like a smothered volcano—we know not when, or where, the flame will burst forth, but we know that death in the most horrid forms threatens us. Some have died, others have become deranged from apprehension, since the South Hampton affair. Can you reflect on the instrument employed for our destruction—that we may trace the *train* as far as *Boston,* & not use your efforts to arrest its course, to make an example of the Author of evil? Your Southern Brethren incurred this curse by no act of their own, they are endeavoring by degrees, & consistently with their safety, & even existence, to remove it. Suffer them to do what they know to be best, & let [not] their Eastern, & Northern Brethren from a false principle of Philanthropy, make the blacks miserable, discontented, & rebellious, & force the whites to *exterminate* them.

William Lloyd Garrison, editor of *The Liberator,* published this contradictory letter which he had received on the front page of his weekly paper. [From *The Liberator,* September 17, 1831, p. 150.]

SIR—I have sometimes heard people say, that if it had not been for the Liberator, the slaves in Virginia would have been quiet. Opinions of this kind are uttered with the greatest gravity and confidence by persons who have never seen the Liberator, and in the absence of all evidence that any one of the persons concerned in the late sanguinary proceedings in Virginia had ever read the paper.

The truth is, that men are too ready to ascribe sudden and violent eruptions of evil to the operation of temporary causes. Every one is more ready to charge any sickness under which he may be suffering to some accident, rather than to a decaying constitution; he is willing to flatter himself that his malady is not deeply rooted in his frame.

There would, perhaps, be some show of justice in charging the recent insurrection to the Liberator, if no other obvious and sufficient causes of such risings could be pointed out, or if this were the first occasion on which slaves had risen against their masters. But, sir, the causes of negro insurrections may be discovered without any deep research,—they obtrude themselves upon our observation.

Negroes, like other men, have a spirit which rebels against tyranny and oppression. It is their wrongs and sufferings which have driven them to the unjustifiable measures which we now lament. Let any unprejudiced person read the law, or observe the practice of slavery in the Southern States, and he will see sufficient causes of insurrections, and will only wonder that they are not more frequent. He will find that men are bought and sold like cattle, that the mother may be torn from the child and carried to a distant region where she will never see his face again, that negroes are compelled to work like brutes, that they are deprived of the produce of their labors, that they are hated and despised and regarded as inferior beings by the whites, that their color is a badge of ignominy, that the laws give them no protection against the insults and injuries of men of a different color from themselves; that the courts of justice are shut against them; that whatever may be their wrongs, they can bring no suit for redress; and that they are subjected to cruel punishments for trifling offences. Would it be strange if a people thus crushed and borne down should entertain feelings of indignation against their oppressors? Let a stranger go into a southern city and observe the squalid appearance and coarse and tattered garments of the blacks, perceive their brutal ignorance, and notice the unfeeling insolence and scorn with which they are treated by the whites, will he wonder that such a population should sometimes become uneasy and troublesome? Let him observe their sullen looks as they slowly retire to their dwellings when the evening bell informs them that they can be tolerated no later in the streets, will he be surprised to learn that they nourish a bitter feeling of hatred against that class which is thus daily interfering with their enjoyments; or that this bell, like the curfew in England which roused in an instant all the rage of the Saxons against their Norman oppressors, should operate in the same manner on the minds of the negroes? Let the stranger then listen to the military music of the armed watch which is kept all night in the city; and in case of an alarm of fire by day or night, let him watch the citizens rushing from their houses armed with muskets and cartridge-boxes, and then let him ask himself whether slaveholders do not anticipate insurrections among their slaves? And as these precautions were taken long before the Liberator was established, may he not conclude that symptoms of disaffection also existed among the slaves before that time?

Other obvious causes of insurrection might easily be pointed out; but I shall only advert to one.—This is a land of freedom. Nothing can prevent the slaves from hearing conversation and declamation of liberty and the rights of man. They perceive our annual celebration on the fourth of July. Can they fail to learn something of its causes? Do not our boastings of our resistance to British oppression sometimes reach their ears? Are they deaf to the sympathising applause with which the accounts of the noble resistance of Poland to Russian despotism, have been received in America? It cannot be. Even if they had less of a human nature than the whites, even if they were not keenly sensible of their wrongs, they would soon learn from their masters how to prize freedom.

But, sir, every one who is at all familiar with ancient or modern history, must be aware that conspiracies and insurrections have always been frequent among slaves. They are the natural fruit of oppression. It would fill volumes to give an account of all the risings of slaves which are recorded in the history of Greece, Rome, South America, the West Indies, and the United States. Hundreds of such cases have probably occurred long before the invention of printing, and in places where newspapers were never circulated. For slaveholders then to ascribe the recent disturbance in Virginia to the Liberator, seems very much like the charge of the wolf against the lamb of muddying the stream from which he was drinking, while she was standing at a point below him. It is as unreasonable to call the Liberator the author of the outrages of the blacks, because it has endeavored to warn the southern people of their danger, as it would be to charge a man with having set fire to your house, because he woke you and told that it was in flames.

O. L.

The Violent Rhetoric of Slavery Days

Slaves, slaveholders, and opponents of slavery all rather casually accepted violence as inseparable from slavery. Slavery's defenders, accustomed to meeting internal threats of upheaval with force, easily established violent rhetoric as the accepted medium for discussing their peculiar institution. Similarly, as abolitionism gained momentum, its leaders relied ever more heavily on stories of brutality, whose enormities they were by no means reluctant to embellish. Vehement resistance to change on the one hand and a sense of imminent divine retribution on the other fostered mutual acceptance of the belief that if slavery were ever to end, it could only be through violence. These fears proved well-founded, as President Lincoln pointed out in his Second Inaugural Address, given during the Civil War.

Fugitive slave Frederick Douglass spoke about slavery's intrinsic need for violence in his "Reception Speech" at Finsbury Chapel, Moorfields, England, May 12, 1846. [From Frederick Douglass, *My Bondage and Freedom* (New York: Miller, Orton & Mulligan, 1855), pp. 410–11.]

The slave-dealer boldly publishes his infamous acts to the world. Of all the things that have been said of slavery to which exception has been taken by slaveholders, this, the charge of cruelty, stands foremost, and yet there is no charge capable of clearer demonstration than that of the most barbarous inhumanity on the part of the slave-holders toward their slaves. And all this is necessary; it is necessary to resort to these cruelties, in order to make the slave a slave, and to keep him a slave. Why, my experience all goes to prove the truth of what you will call a marvelous proposition, that the better you treat a slave, the more you destroy his value as a slave, and enhance the probability of his eluding the grasp of the slaveholder; the more kindly you treat him, the more wretched you make him, while you keep him in the condition of a slave. My experience, I say, confirms the truth of this proposition. When I was treated exceedingly ill;

when my back was being scourged daily; when I was whipped within an inch of my life—life was all I cared for. "Spare my life," was my continual prayer. When I was looking for the blow about to be inflicted upon my head, I was not thinking of my liberty; it was my life. But, as soon as the blow was not to be feared, then came the longing for liberty. If a slave has a bad master, his ambition is to get a better; when he gets a better, he aspires to have the best; and when he gets the best, he aspires to be his own master. But the slave must be brutalized to keep him as a slave. The slaveholder feels this necessity. I admit this necessity. If it be right to hold slaves at all, it is right to hold them in the only way in which they can be held; and this can be done only by shutting out the light of education from their minds, and brutalizing their persons.

"The whip, the chain, the gag, the thumb-screw, the bloodhound, the stocks, and all the other bloody paraphernalia of the slave system are indispensably necessary to the relation of master and slave. The slave must be subjected to these, or he ceases to be a slave. Let him know that the whip is burned; that the fetters have been turned to some useful and profitable employment; that the chain is no longer for his limbs; that the bloodhound is no longer to be put upon his track; that his master's authority over him is no longer to be enforced by taking his life—and immediately he walks out from the house of bondage and asserts his freedom as a man. The slaveholder finds it necessary to have these implements to keep the slave in bondage; finds it necessary to be able to say, "Unless you do so and so; unless you do as I bid you—I will take away your life!"

The white point of view. *Memorial of the Citizens of Charleston to the Senate and House of Representatives of the State of South Carolina, 1822.* [From Phillips, *Plantation and Frontier,* II, 103–5.]

At a moment of anxiety and in a season of deep solicitude, resulting from the recent discovery of a projected insurrection among our colored population, your Memorialists submit to you the following considerations:

Under the influence of mild and generous feelings, the owners of slaves in our state were rearing up a system, which extended many privileges to our negroes; afforded them greater protection; relieved them from numerous restraints; enabled them to assemble without the presence of a white person for the purpose of social intercourse or religious worship; yielding to them the facilities of acquiring most of the comforts and many of the luxuries of improved society; and what is of more importance, affording them means of enlarging their minds and extending their information; a system, whose establishment many persons could not reflect on without concern, and whose rapid extension, the experienced among us could not observe but "with fear and trembling," nevertheless, a system which met the approbation of by far the greater number of our citizens, who exulted in what they termed the progress of liberal ideas upon the subject of slavery, whilst many good and pious persons fondly cherished the expectation that our negroes would be influenced in their conduct towards their owners by sentiments of affection and gratitude.

The tranquility and good order manifested for a time among the slaves, induced your memorialists to regard the extension of their privileges, in a favourable light, and to entertain the hope that as they were more indulged, they would become more satisfied with their condition and more attached to the whites.

It becomes us, however painful it may prove, to sacrifice feeling to reason, and mistaken compassion to a stern policy, and expel from our territory every free person of color, that we may extinguish at once every gleam of hope which the slaves may indulge of ever being free—and that we may proceed to govern them on the only principle that can maintain slavery, the "principle of fear."

William Lloyd Garrison's reaction to the news of Nat Turner's Rebellion expressed this abolitionist theme of impending divine retribution for the sin of slaveholding. [From *The Liberator*, September 3, 1831, p. 143.]

What we have so long predicted,—at the peril of being stigmatized as an alarmist and declaimer,—has commenced its fulfilment. The first step of the earthquake, which is ultimately to shake down the fabric of oppression, leaving not one stone upon another, has been made. The first drops of blood, which are but the prelude to a deluge from the gathering clouds, have fallen. The first flash of the lightening, which is to smite and consume, has been felt. The first wailings of a bereavement, which is to clothe the earth in sackcloth, have broken upon our ears.

In the first number of the Liberator, we alluded to the hour of vengeance in the following lines:

> Wo if it come with storm, and blood, and fire,
>> When midnight darkness veils the earth and sky!
> Wo to the innocent babe—the guilty sire—
>> Mother and daughter—friends of kindred tie!
> Stranger and citizen alike shall die!

Red-handed Slaughter his revenge shall feed,
  And Havoc yell his ominous death-cry,
  And wild Despair in vain for mercy plead—
  While hell itself shall shrink and sicken at the deed!

Read the account of the insurrection in Virginia, and say whether our prophecy be not fulfilled. What was poetry—imagination—in January, is now a bloody reality. "Wo to the innocent babe—to mother and daughter!" Is it not true? Turn again to the record of slaughter! Whole families have been cut off—not a mother, not a daughter, not a babe left. Dreadful retaliation! "The dead bodies of white and black lying just as they were slain, unburied"—the oppressor and the oppressed equal at last in death—what a spectacle!

[From President Abraham Lincoln's "Second Inaugural Address," March 4, 1865.]

Fondly do we hope—fervently do we pray—that this mighty scourge of war may speedily pass away. Yet, if God wills that it continue, until all the wealth piled by the bond-man's two hundred and fifty years of unrequited toil shall be sunk, and until every drop of blood drawn with the lash, shall be paid by another drawn with the sword, as was said three thousand years ago, so still it must be said "the judgments of the Lord, are true and righteous altogether."

☞ 3 ☜

BULLIES AND MOBS

Emancipation presented whites with the task of finding a substitute system of caste control. They no longer owned blacks, and this cost whites the total command inherent in property rights at the same time as it relieved them of a vested interest in the blacks' physical well-being. These new factors, combined with the slave heritage of violence, pointed to a continued reliance on physical coercion and more serious punishments for violating the code of social etiquette governing race relations.

Southern states, where most blacks lived, gradually evolved systems of legal restraint: jim crow laws to prevent social equality, disfranchise-ment to remove black political influence, and agricultural serfdom to recreate the plantation system as closely as possible. During the tran-sition to this new order, extralegal organizations such as the Ku Klux Klan underscored white determination to keep blacks in their place through supplemental programs of outright violence and ritual terror. Although the fortunes of the Klan itself have subsequently waxed and waned, murder, beating, and property destruction have been used and threatened to extract respect from blacks and to squelch black aspirations. Since the closing years of the nineteenth century, lynch-ings have occurred with declining frequency. Yet the murders of civil rights workers in the 1960s and such atrocities as the ritual castration of an unsuspecting Alabama Negro by members of the Klan in 1957 indicate that some whites still accept terrorism as a means of social control.

When blacks moved to Northern cities, interracial violence moved with them. Isolated bombing incidents and mob scenes short of riots have been prompted by what whites regarded as black encroachment on their preserves. And the high incidence of crimes committed against the person—assault, rape, and homicide—by blacks against blacks indicates a continuation of the tradition of violence turned inward.

In the 1950s blacks began to supplement less visible assaults against the legal caste system with direct social action, and the "civil rights movement" became part of everyone's vocabulary, as did *Brown* vs. *Board of Education,* Little Rock, Birmingham, the Reverend Martin Luther King, Jr., cattle-prod, and George C. Wallace. Negroes boycotted bus lines and retail stores, sat in at segregated lunch counters, tried to use such tax-supported facilities as courthouses, libraries, and schools, tried to vote, and marched on city streets and rural highways. Whites reacted with predictably violent determination. A steady diet of shocking news followed and became common fare. Later, when blacks began lashing out against Northern ghettos, most whites tended to forget who the perpetrators of civil rights violence really had been. Having blurred distinctions between types of violence, they reasserted anti-Negro prejudices, now called "white backlash."

Out of this history of violent deeds have come violent words. Many spokesmen for both sides go beyond mere justification to embrace violence. Many whites have insisted that blacks won't keep in line without force and that especially if they continue to rape white women, they must be lynched (although statistics show that homicide, not rape, has been the primary cause of lynchings). An increasing number of blacks insist that, while they are prepared to defend themselves, they did not start the violence; with a mixture of eagerness and resignation they accept the necessity of taking what they desire by force. Since both sides talk in terms of retaliation, armed conflict— of course in a "defensive" or "preventive" war—is made more likely.

The KKK During Reconstruction

Following the Civil War freedmen, the Federal government, and a good number of sympathetic whites worked in a variety of ways to facilitate the entrance of ex-slaves into American life. Most Southern whites resented these efforts, which they perceived as attempts to effect social upheaval. Their old insecurities activated, some of them organized "secret" societies designed to allay their own fears and prevent black progress by violence and intimidation. Among these ritualistic terrorist societies was the Ku Klux Klan. Reports of its activities disturbed key Northern Congressmen, who investigated the Klan in 1870–71. An excerpt is given below from the testimony of Henry Hamlin (colored) to the Alabama Sub-Committee at Huntsville, Alabama, October 12, 1871. [From Joint Committee to Inquire into the Condition of Affairs in the Late Insurrectionary States, *The Ku-*

Klux Conspiracy, 13 vols. (Washington, D.C.: Government Printing Office, 1872), IX, 857–59.]

Huntsville, Alabama, 1871

Question. Where do you live?

Answer. I live in this county—Madison County.

Question. Have you ever been whipped by the Ku-Klux?

Answer. Yes, sir.

Question. When?

Answer. About three years ago.

Question. Where?

Answer. Down about three or five miles, at Trinity, down below De-catur.

Question. What county is that in?

Answer. In this county.

Question. What were you whipped for?

Answer. I couldn't tell you what it was for.

Question. Who whipped you?

Answer. I didn't know none of them. . . .

Question. What did the men have on over their faces and bodies?

Answer. White gowns, that came down to their knees, and scolloped over the face; you couldn't see his face, and he had a high hat on the head.

Question. Was the face painted?

Answer. No, sir; they had the face covered so we couldn't see. They whipped the first one pretty badly.

Question. What did they whip him with?

Answer. With one of these pistol-holsters that comes around. They let him down and whipped him. They laid down a fence-rail, and tied his hands and feet to it, and seven men whipped him at once. They whipped him so bad he couldn't turn over, and he couldn't get home.

Question. Did they have hickory?

Answer. No, sir; just leather straps.

Question. What did they whip you with?

Answer. Leather straps.

Question. How many lashes?

Answer. I couldn't tell you. I never was whipped so much in all the days of my life.

Question. Did it make the blood run?

Answer. Yes, sir; it blistered me all over. I sometimes feel the pain coming back in my back now; I never have got well from it; it hurt me so bad.

Question. How many of you colored people were whipped by that party?

Answer. There wasn't but four.

Question. What time of night was this?

Answer. I think it was about 11 o'clock in the night.

Question. Did they accuse you colored men of voting the radical ticket?

Answer. Yes, sir; a heap of them did. They were talking and trying to make me tell something about the Union League they had up here. After they found out I came from Huntsville they wanted me to tell something about the Union League; I told them I didn't know anything about it; they said, "It had been down at Decatur"; I knew they had a gathering down at Decatur once; he said I was along in the crowd, he was told; I told him I wasn't there, that I knew they went down there; he tried to make me tell about some man that was at the head of it; I don't know who it was now; they tried to make me tell; I told them I didn't know who was at the head, and I didn't know. Then they whipped me and whipped me, and then I wouldn't tell, and one of them thought he would take up a fence rail and kill me, but the captain of the Ku-Klux said, "No, let him up; don't hurt him any more; you have done enough to him." One said, "Damn me if I don't kill him," and the captain got sort o' mad because they wanted to kill me, and he wouldn't let them; he said no, I should not be killed, and he didn't go to kill me. Then they let me up and took another man; that man is out here now; they whipped him; he would raise up his head every once in a while when they were whipping him, and one of them had brass spurs on, and he struck him in his face with the spur; he struck him on the top of the head about that deep, (two inches); they took two bones out of that man's head, and he bled a great deal. After he got well, as he thought, and got the wound cured, it broke out again, and the doctor took two bones out of it since.

Question. What did they tell you you must do when they left you?

Answer. They told us we must go home and go to work on the railroad, and be good boys, and when they came across us again they wouldn't hurt us; but that other man that got away, named Scruggs, they told him they would make his coffin, and set it in his house, for they were going to kill him.

Question. Kill him for what?

Answer. They didn't say. They said he had been talking some big talk, they heard, and they were going to kill him, and they shouldn't talk such big talk; that we had got so here that we thought we could rule this country.

Question. Did they call themselves Ku-Klux?

Answer. Yes, sir; they said they were just from hell; that they had had no water for three or four days at a time; they said God sent them down here, and they were going to rule us.

Senator "Pitchfork" Ben Tillman was a colorful South Carolina demagogue who spent much of his time on the Senate floor defending Southern racism. In this speech he told about the origins of Negro disfranchisement. [From the *Congressional Record*, Vol. 33, pt. 3 (56th Congress, 1st Session, February 26, 1900) p. 2245.]

Let me tell you how we were situated in our State. We had a hundred and twenty-five thousand negroes of voting age and we had a hundred thousand whites. Now, can you lift yourselves over the fence with your boot straps and beat that by honest methods? Yet you stood up here and insisted that we must give these people a "free vote and a fair count." They had it for eight years, as long as the bayonets stood there, and in 1876 they sent more bayonets, because we had got the devil in us by that time and we did not care whether we had any government. We preferred to have a United States Army officer rather than a government by carpetbaggers and thieves and scallywags and scoundrels, who had stolen everything in sight and had mortgaged posterity; who had run their felonious paws into the pockets of posterity by issuing bonds.

When that happened, we took the government away. We stuffed ballot boxes. We shot them. We are not ashamed of it.

Intimidation was also intended to discourage blacks from owning land. [From Cornelius McBride, white witness, 1871, *The Ku-Klux Conspiracy*, XI, 335.]

There is this state of affairs there: As a general rule a man is very unpopular with his neighbors who will sell land to colored people; and then a colored man is in danger if he buys land. In Winston County a dozen men were whipped, and the only charge against them was that they had bought land. A colored man of the name of William Coleman, in Louisville, Winston County, bought eighty acres of land, and just after buying the land a body of disguised men came there and took him out of his house and nearly killed him, left him for dead in the road. The only charge they made against him was the buying of this land, and they threatened at the same time to kill the man who had sold it to him.

Lynching

Lynching has been associated in American mythology with frontier justice—swift, final, though sometimes misguided. But western states accounted for only 8 per cent of the 4,716 lynchings reported in the United States from 1882 to 1946. (This information is from *The 1947 Negro Year Book* [Tuskegee Institute: The Department of Records and Research, 1947], pp. 308–9.) During this same period Southern mobs lynched 3,905 persons, or 83 per cent of the total, of

whom 3,245 were black. Lynching has declined since its heyday in
the 1890s (the lynching of whites has virtually stopped since the mid-
1920s), but from 1927 to 1946 some 178 Negro lynchings were reported. Though whites have defended the practice most often as
just punishment for rapists, only one of every five lynch victims was
even charged with this offense; undoubtedly a number of these were
innocent. Two of every five lynch victims were alleged homicides,
while the remainder died for deeds ranging from felonious assault
to "disputing with a white man." Lynching focused the hostilities
of a mob, often of riot proportions, on a single human object, who
become a symbol, an actor in a violent racial drama.

The scenes described in the following news story could easily be
associated with any lynching. "Fred Alexander Dies at Stake," Leavenworth, Kansas. [From *The Denver Republican,* January 16, 1901.]

Then again a sledge hammer was called into action and in five
minutes the heavy lock had been broken off. A fierce yell, the yell of a
beast brought to bay, issued from the cell. Outside the tension was
so great that strong men filled the room with hysterical laughter.

Outside the crowd was yelling in a manner never before heard in
the city of Leavenworth.

Inside the cell rushed those who were nearest the door.

The mob issued in a moment dragging the fiend by the coat collar.
He had been struck over the head with a hammer, but was still conscious.

Men fought to get at him. These infuriated humans struck savagely
at him and hit only his captors, who guarded him well.

"Don't hurt him," they cried.

"We'll burn him," was the response.

Outside the stockade the crowd surged. Alexander and his captors
were surrounded by a solid wall of human flesh. Across Third street
and up the hill into the court house yard they dragged him. Then
they stopped.

"Confess before we harm you," said they.

"I have nothing to confess," cried Alexander. "I am innocent. I am
dying for what another man did. I see lots of my friends here. They
know I did not do it. If I had been guilty I would have said so at
the penitentiary and would have stayed there for life.

"The warden told me so. The policeman told me so. Would not I
have told them if I was guilty?"

He did not know the town was bent on lynching, that all minds
were made up that he had committed a crime that could only be
avenged with his blood.

"You lie," they cried, and one huge fellow, filled more with the lust for blood than with the feelings of a human, struck him in the forehead with his fist three times. This seemed not to have the slightest effect on the negro. He was turning white.

When he talked his voice was steady. He spoke with the resignation of a man who sees only before him death, slow, perhaps, but certain, and was prepared to meet it in its most awful form.

When he had finished talking, a move was made for a large cotton-wood tree in the northeast corner of the courthouse yard. He was backed up against it, and a chain was hunted for. One could not be found, and while they waited Alexander was given another chance to confess.

"My God, men," he cried in his agony. "I have told you that I'm innocent. I can't tell you any more. I didn't do it."

"He lies! Burn him!" cried the mob.

"Take him where he committed the murder," suggested one.

The suggestion met with instant approval, and the crowd, carrying the negro and his captors, started for Fourth street. There were many wagons standing about and into one they threw him. As soon as his guards got in the wagon was started for the vicinity of Lawrence avenue and Spruce, followed on the run by the crowd.

At a quarter past 5 o'clock Alexander was brought to the scene of the murder of Pearl Forbes, at the corner of Lawrence avenue and Spruce street. The exact spot where the murdered girl was found was located by the leaders of the crowd, and there a semi-circle was formed.

Alexander was brought up in a wagon with a dozen men. The wagon was stopped in front of the ravine and surrounded by the crowd, the leader of the men who had Alexander called for silence.

The roar ceased and Alexander was shoved forward for the crowd to gaze at. A howl went up which was quickly hushed as the prisoner raised his shackled hands and began to speak.

Twice he started and the crowd drowned his trembling voice.

"You're going to kill me, whatever I say," he said, "but you men are wrong. I want to tell you right now you've got the wrong man.

"I did not do that and some day you men here will run up against the man who did. I know it ain't no use to say so, for you're going to kill me, but I did not do it."

The men standing beside him shoved Alexander from the wagon and the roar of the crowd drowned every other sound. He was quickly dragged down the embankment to the pile of wood, with his hands still shackled, and there bound to the stake.

Long before the wagon containing the doomed man arrived at the place a crowd gathered. Determined men, as they approached, carried rails and boards. Several seized railroad irons and carried them to the ravine. The spot chosen for the stake was the exact one on which Pearl Forbes' body was found the morning of November 7.

The first thing done was to plant the railroad iron upright in the mud. This was made fast to cross irons firmly bound to the upright iron with wire. Around the improvised stake, boards and wood was piled. To this the man was dragged and chained in a standing position to the upright railroad iron. Chains and irons were wrapped about him, with his hands still shackled fast to the post. Coal oil was then poured over him and the match touched to him.

Before the match was applied John Forbes, the father of the murdered girl, stepped up to Alexander and said:

"Are you guilty of murdering my daughter?"

"I don't know what you have me here for," said the doomed man. Forbes replied, "For killing my girl on this very spot."

"Mr. Forbes, if that's your name, you have the wrong man."

"Burn him! burn him!" cried the crowd.

"Gentlemen, you have got lots of time," said Alexander. "You are burning an innocent man. You took advantage of me. You gave me no show. Can I see my mother?"

A man in the crowd called for the mother of the negro, but she was not in the crowd. He then said:

"Will you let me shake hands with all of my friends?"

"You have no friends in this crowd, you damned beast," said one of the men in charge of the negro.

"If you have anything to say, do so in a hurry."

Another man then stepped up and said to Alexander: "Make your peace with your God, nigger, for you will surely die."

Coal oil was then applied for the second time, and while it was being done Alexander called to friends in the crowd and bade them good-by. He did not seem to realize that he was to be burned at the stake and talked rationally until John Forbes, the father of the murdered girl, lighted the match.

Again Alexander was asked to make a confession, but the negro replied that he had nothing to say.

As the flames leaped about him, Alexander turned ghastly pale and then for the first time realized that his death was near. He clasped his hands together and began to swing to and fro, while the crowd yelled.

In less than five minutes he was hanging limp and lifeless by the chains that bound him.

As soon as the crowd saw that life was extinct, it began to slowly disperse. There were hundreds of the more morbid, however, who stayed to the last.

Men kept piling on wood until about 7 o'clock, when the flames were allowed to die down.

From 6 to 8 o'clock there was a continuous stream of people going to the scene of the burning. These were persons who had been unable to get away from their work in the afternoon, but were determined not to miss the awful spectacle.

When the fire had died down sufficiently to allow the crowd to approach what remained of Alexander, there was a wild scramble to obtain relics. Bits of charred flesh, pieces of chain, scraps of wood— everything that could possibly serve as a souvenir, was seized on with morbid avidity by the eager people.

Once again, from the floor of the United States Senate, the notori- ous South Carolina Senator "Pitchfork" Ben Tillman justified the use of violence against blacks. His version of lynching follows. [From *Congressional Record*, Vol. 36, pt. 2, (59th Cong., 2nd Sess., January 21, 1907), p. 1441.]

Have I ever advocated lynch law at any time or at any place? I answer on my honor, "Never!" I have justified it for one crime, and one only, and I have consistently and persistently maintained that attitude for the last fourteen years. As governor of South Carolina I proclaimed that, although I had taken the oath of office to support the law and enforce it, I would lead a mob to lynch any man, black or white, who had ravished a woman, black or white. This is my attitude calmly and deliberately taken, and justified by my conscience in the sight of God.

Mr. President, the Senator from Wisconsin speaks of "lynching bees." As far as lynching for rape is concerned, the word is a misnomer. When stern and sad-faced white men put to death a creature in human form who has deflowered a white woman, there is nothing of the "bee" about it. There is more of the feeling of participating as mourner at a funeral. They have avenged the greatest wrong, the blackest crime in all the category of crimes, and they have done it, not so much as an act of retribution in behalf of the victim as a duty and as a warning as to what any man may expect who shall repeat the offense. They are looking to the protection of their own loved ones.

On May 9, 1930, a mob of irate whites in Sherman, Texas, was refused access to an incarcerated Negro accused of assaulting a white woman, so they burned down the courthouse where he had been locked in a vault. After the fire, members of this mob blasted open the vault, which blast probably killed the man, and dragged his body

through the streets of Sherman. A young black maid describes what
she saw that night. [From a press story by Roscoe Dunjee, *The Pittsburgh Courier,* May 24, 1930. Selections from *The Pittsburgh Courier*
are reprinted by permission of the managing editor of that newspaper.]

"My boss wanted to go down to look at the mob. When he loaded
his wife and little baby up in the car I refused to stay home. He told
me to get in and sit way back in the rear seat between his wife and
daughter. I spent three hours peeping out of that car.

"When we arrived on the street by the courthouse the crowd was
singing 'Happy Days Are Here Again.' They sang other songs, but
I do not recall them. I was struck most by the grotesque and unseemly
notion of these human butchers singing 'Happy Days Are Here Again.'
Women with babies in their arms cried and shouted, and I never in
my life heard such vile and profane language as was dinned into my
ears, seemingly from everywhere.

"I was horrified when they finally dumped the charred body of a
man out of the building. The men and boys quickly got a chain and
fastened the body to a car and dragged it through the streets of the
colored section, ending at the Goodson building.

"A small cottonwood tree was used as a gallows for the already
dead man. The Goodson store was broken into with axes and the
furnishings were chopped up to make a fire. I saw the boys as they
passed cigars, cigarets and perfume to the men and women."

A Chicago minister comments on lynching. [From *The Denver
Republican,* June 29, 1903.]

"I am no advocate of lynching or of mob law, but I would rather
see a community wrought to the highest pitch over crimes that would
seem impossible this side of hell than to remain apathetic," was the
declaration of Rev. Dr. W. A. Bartlett at the First Congregational
church to-day in a prelude on "lynching from another point of view."
Dr. Bartlett said:

"I have seen so many sermons, editorials and resolutions denounc-
ing lynching and mob law that one gets the impression that the citizens
who hang or burn the destroyers of life, home and all that is held
sacred by womanhood are the offenders, rather than the monster whom
they destroy."

[Mrs. W. H. Felton to the Editor, *Atlanta Journal,* November 15,
1898.]

LYNCH 1,000 WEEKLY, DECLARES MRS. FELTON

In reply to your telegram concerning . . . my address before the Agricultural society at Tybee one year ago last August, I here repeat what was said at Tybee and re-affirm the same.

Addressing farmers, I said the crying need of women on farms is security in their lives and homes.

It is a disgrace in a free country when rape and violence are public reproach, and the best part of God's creation are trembling and afraid to be left alone in their homes.

With due respect to your politics, I say that when you take the negro into your embraces on election day to control his vote and use liquor to befuddle his understanding and make him believe he is your man and brother, when you honey-snuggle him at the polls and make him familiar with dirty tricks in politics, so long will lynching prevail, because the cause will grow and increase with every election, and when there is not enough religion in the pulpit to organize a crusade against this sin nor justice in the courthouse to promptly punish the crime, nor manhood enough in the nation to put a sheltering arm about innocence and virtue, if it requires lynching to protect woman's dearest possession from ravening, drunken human beasts, then I say lynch a thousand a week if it is necessary.

Why do people participate in lynch mobs? Dr. Arthur Raper studied this question under the auspices of the Southern Commission on the Study of Lynching. [From Arthur F. Raper, *The Tragedy of Lynching* (Chapel Hill: The University of North Carolina Press, 1933), pp. 47–48. Reprinted by permission of the publisher.]

. . . The mobs of 1930 had about 75,000 members—men and women and children who went out to kill, or to look on sympathetically while others killed. And not one of these so-called onlookers is morally or legally guiltless: Their very presence directly complicated the task of the peace officers, and emboldened the active lynchers by reflecting to them the community's general approval.

While these seventy-five thousand people were members of actual mobs but one day in the year, they were most probably mob-minded every day in the year. Millions of others were mob-disposed, and under provocation would have joined a mob, killing or standing sympathetically by while others killed. Mobs do not come out of the nowhere; they are the logical outgrowths of dominant assumptions and prevalent thinking. Lynchings are not the work of men suddenly possessed of a strange madness; they are the logical issues of prejudice and lack of respect for law and personality, plus a sadistic desire to participate in the excitement of mob trials and the brutalities of mob torture and murder.

The anti-social and inhumane desires which find expression in lynchings often serve as socializing forces within the white group. Not infrequently more unanimity can be had on a lynching than on any other subject. Lynchings tend to minimize social and class distinctions between white plantation owners and white tenants, mill owners and textile workers, Methodists and Baptists, and so on. This prejudice against the Negro forms a common meeting place for whites, adds to race antagonism, and further reveals the essentially negative and craven character of the lynchers and their apoligists.

A most baffling aspect of the situation is suggested by the fact that the lynchers often are not content with the death of their victims. They torture, mutilate, and burn. One is forced to the conclusion that their deeper motivation is a desire not for the just punishment of the accused so much as for an opportunity to participate in protracted brutalities.

Integration and Terror

Lynching is mob activity directed toward a single individual who has outraged a community; often mob action directs collective hostility toward groups of individuals who are openly assaulting the established social order. When the mere threat of violence has lost its power to deter blacks from seeking an education, attempting to attend white schools, moving into all-white housing, or generally protesting against the pattern of segregation, white mobs have resorted to actual violence in an effort to "keep them in their place." In this selection, the Congressional investigating committee heard about the use of terror in 1871 to keep freedmen from receiving any schooling. Cornelius McBride migrated from Ireland to Cincinnati, then left to teach in a Negro school in Mississippi. After eleven months in Chickasaw County, he had been chased from his house during the night, stripped, and beaten. [From *Ku-Klux Conspiracy*, XI, 326–29.]

Question. Black-gum switches?

Answer. Yes, sir; a peculiar kind of stick, which stings and raises the flesh where it hits. One of them took the bundle of switches and commenced to whip me. They said they were going to give me a hundred each. I do not know how many men there were; I counted only five around me, but I believe there were more than a dozen there. They agreed to give me a hundred lashes each. One man gave me a hundred and then handed the bundle of switches to another, who gave me about seventy-five. He said he had given me seventy-five when I escaped from them. I asked them while they were whipping me what I had done to merit that treatment. They said I wanted to make these niggers equal with the white men; that this was a white man's country. They said, "God damn you! Don't you know this is a white man's country?" I said, "The white people in the neighborhood are satisfied with my conduct and the manner I have been conducting the school here. They have shown it by selecting me to take charge of their Sunday school." They said, "Yes, God damn you, that is the worst feature in it, having a nigger teacher to teach the white school on Sunday!"

❊   ❊   ❊

Three miles from where I live, Mr. Burt Moore lives. He is a southern man; he was a great secessionist before the war and during the war; but since the war he has accepted the new state of affairs. He is an old man and a poor man, and he opened a colored school in order to make something to support himself and family. He has accepted the situation, and is now a republican, and has become unpopular through voting the republican ticket. They put a notice on his door to this effect: "Mr. Burt Moore: We do not want to hurt you, but you must stop teaching this school." He continued to teach the school, though. The colored people had come out of their fields and erected the schoolhouse themselves; and just one week after they had completed it, it was burned down.

The question of educating blacks still agitates white supremacists; in mid-twentieth century the issue involves black children attending schools with white children. In 1966 photographer Jack Cantrell covered a school integration disturbance for a Memphis newspaper in his nearby hometown, Grenada, Mississippi. He soon discovered how vehement and indiscriminate white hostility could be. [From the *Memphis Press-Scimitar*, September 12, 1966. Selections from the *Memphis Press-Scimitar* are reprinted by permission of the managing editor of that newspaper.]

When Charles Goodman (*Press-Scimitar* reporter) and I arrived down the street from the school, the first thing we saw were Negro students being hit and kicked by a mob of white people. There must have been at least 400 whites in the mob. It was an angry mob.

The Negro children were crying. One Negro boy, about 12, had apparently been kicked. He was crying and limping.

A white man said to him: "Now, are you going to come back to school here again?"

The boy told the man that he didn't want to go to school there in the first place. He said, "My parents made me come."

Charlie and I walked down the sidewalk toward the school. Somebody in the crowd hollered to me: "If you want to get out of here, you better give us the camera."

We had already passed them, so we kept walking. When we got in front of the school, Capt. W. C. Turner, the Grenada police chief, said to us: "Boy, haven't you read the paper? We ran a piece in the paper saying there would be no pictures taken down here. You'll have to get off the school property and get across the street."

He said we couldn't stand on the sidewalk in front of the school because he said it was school property. He said we couldn't stand in the street in front of the school because that is also school property.

So we went across the street. While we were standing there Jim Reid (*Press-Scimitar* photographer on special assignment with United Press International) walked up and we stood there talking a minute or so.

We saw two or three more Negro boys and girls walking down the side-walk leaving school. Suddenly they were surrounded by at least 80 people. Three or four of the men hit and kicked the children. The rest of the mob cursed the kids.

One of the men yanked a branch off a tree and hit one of the Negro girls over the head.

They were out of our camera range at the time and we didn't want to go down where they were.

About five or 10 minutes passed and nothing happened. The Negro children stayed inside the school, apparently afraid to come out.

The crowd seemed to grow impatient.

That's when they decided to mob the photographers and newsmen in the area. The crowd was so worked up that the people didn't care who they attacked.

They started running in my direction, but I didn't think they were going to get me.

Before I knew it they were on top of me.

I was surrounded. Someone blurted out: "You better give us that damn camera."

I said, "Man, I haven't even taken a picture."

They reached up and jerked the camera from around my neck. I grabbed the strap and swung and hit somebody on the head with it. That was the last I saw of my camera.

Although they already had the camera, they still jumped me, hitting me with their fists. I saw several broom sticks lashing out at me. I was hit on the side of the face with the broomsticks. I couldn't count the fists coming at me. There must have been about 10 people hitting me and a big crowd was looking on. They were laughing and hollering. I don't know what they were hollering because I was too busy trying to defend myself.

There was no place to run. They were all around me.

The next thing I knew I was on my back in the middle of the street. They stomped and kicked me. I fought to my feet and I started swinging wildly.

I was so completely dazed and swinging so wildly that I hit the deputy sheriff right square in the mouth. He looked at me, and a city policeman said to me: "What are you doing hitting him, he's a sheriff!"

I told the man I was sorry—that I didn't know who I was swinging for.

By this time the mob had left me and I saw them mobbing Jim.

The following housing clash in Chicago shortly after World War II has been replicated often in northern cities. [Story by Hugh Gardner, in the *Pittsburgh Courier*, December 14, 1946.]

A mob of whites, variously estimated at between 1,000 and 1,500 persons, demonstrated here Thursday evening at Airport Project Homes in an attempt to prevent two war veterans from moving into the project provided by the Federal Government for former servicemen and their families.

During the demonstration eight persons were injured, six of them from among the nearly 500 police sent by Major Edward J. Kelly to enforce the CHA order to permit all veterans, regardless of race or color, to move into the project on the basis of greatest need. One of the officers struck was Police Lieut. Anthony De Grazio.

The veterans, John R. Fort, 29, of 5952 South Parkway, and Letholian Waddell, 20, of 5009 Dearborn, were not among the injured. However, two automobiles, one owned by Dr. Homer Jack, executive secretary of the Chicago Council Against Racial and Religious Discrimination, and that of Kenneth C. Kennedy, national commander of the United Negro Allied Veterans of America, were overturned.

Fort and Waddell were among nine colored families certified for occupancy in the project. On Friday, although the demonstration at the housing project had subsided, and approximately 200 policemen were still in the area on patrol duty, a project spokesman said all remaining colored families eligible for apartments had withdrawn their names and returned their keys and leases.

The flareup occurred in front of 4126 and 4128 W. Sixtieth Place, where the vets showed up with their furnishings. They were met by a surging mob of jeering whites, mostly women, and youngsters apparently in their teens. The six police and two newspaper men were struck with thrown stones and the cars were upset.

Only the presence of the police kept the angry crowd from damaging the property. Up until Saturday night tension in the area was presumed to be running high and Fort and Waddell, keeping their words that they "would stay to fight this to a finish" came and left their homes under police escort. On Friday evening a crude fiery cross was burned at Sixty-first and Kedvale Avenue.

It was during the resulting melee when police attempted to scatter the mob that eight persons were sent to the hospital. Following the evacuation of the premises by "squatter" white veterans, several weeks ago, it was learned that colored veterans would be allowed occupancy.

[Associated Press, September 16, 1963.] The following two selections are reprinted by permission of the Associated Press.

Aniston, Ala.—Two Negro ministers were beaten Sunday as they apparently attempted to desegregate the public library, police said.

The two were attacked by a crowd of about 100 white persons as they walked up the library steps.

The two, Rev. Quitun Reynolds and Rev. W. B. McClain, managed to escape, police said.

[Associated Press, September 15, 1963.]

Birmingham, Ala.—"The love that forgives" was the Sunday school lesson Sunday at the 16th Street Baptist Church. It was never finished.

A bomb exploded there and twisted the lesson into an experience of confusion, terror and death.

Who knows on what part the four Negro children were reading when they were killed, their bodies hit by flying glass and mortar?

Maybe they had reached the end of the lesson, with a Bible passage from Matthew: "But I say unto you, love your enemies."

The children were meeting in various parts of the church—some were in the basement, some in the main room, and others in an adjacent Sunday school building.

The four killed were in the basement, where a clock is stopped at 10:25.

Shattered windows, large pieces of mortar, and a broken marble plaque commemorating the founding of the church in 1873 are mute testimony to the destruction there.

Up the steps, in the main room, where church services are regularly held for a congregation of 750, the clock is stopped at 10:22.

Glass is scattered on the wooden pews, over the piano and organ, on the pulpit. The organ pipes were left intact.

Behind the pulpit is a little room—the pastor's—which is strewn with litter, twisted tables and mortar. A phone there rings constantly, answered by a church deacon.

"No, we don't know the names of who was killed. I'm going down to the hospital soon. Don't you worry," he says softly.

Outside, Negroes who live near the church stand around quietly, watching the parade of shotgun-armed policemen, firemen and reporters as they step among shattered glass and stones.

M. W. Pippen looks first at the church and then his store, Social Cleaners, which he owns with his brother. The store damage runs in the thousands of dollars.

But the damage to his heart is more.

"My grandbaby was one of those killed," he says.

"Eleven years old. I helped pull the rocks off her. I got one of her shoes in there," he motions his head toward the inside of his shattered building.

"You know how I feel, I feel like blowing the whole town up. Weak-minded people, that's who brought it on."

Two other stores and a contracting company office were shattered by the blast. Apartment rooms above the stores shuddered. Their windows were knocked out. Four cars were destroyed by the impact and flying rocks.

Groups of Negroes on the corners were dispersed and driven several blocks away by helmeted policemen, just to discourage any possible rioting. But they are quiet. They watch.

The Negro community is angry now, police have no doubt. Many Negroes will tell you that. The police chief has asked for help from the state troopers.

Said Capt. Jack Warren, who with three men, was the first on the scene after the bombing:

"The crowd came from nowhere. Man, they were mad, mad! I wouldn't have given you 15 cents for my life. I've seen a lot of these things. I begged them on the bullhorn, but it didn't do much good."

Capt. Warren said many Negroes started throwing rocks at his men, but none were hit. "A Negro Civil Defense captain came along just in time to help calm the angry crowd," he said.

"We could have had a terrible thing."

[United Press International, September 16, 1963.]

The bombing of a church Sunday marked at least the 21st time in eight years that Birmingham Negroes have been bomb victims.

But Sunday was the first time anyone was killed by the blasts. Four died Sunday and the 21 injured exceeded by one the total injured in all the 20 previous bombings.

Since the bombings began in 1955, the main targets have been Negro churches, the home of integration leader the Rev. Fred L. Shuttlesworth and the homes of Negroes moving into a white section that came to be known as "dynamite Hill."

"Let's Learn His Language"

By the 1960s black Americans were no longer in the mood to refrain from violence. Too many, even among those who had attained fame and fortune in white society, had bitter personal encounters which forcefully reminded them of their assigned subordinate position. To be sure many Negro leaders counseled patience and restraint even in the face of such atrocities as the Birmingham church bombing. And so Martin Luther King continued to march, preaching nonviolence, and the NAACP continued its legal battles. But other leaders simply lost all faith in the good will of whites and stopped believing they would voluntarily relinquish their superior status and power. Many of these leaders drew their inspiration from the African revolutions which were gradually expelling European colonial rule from that continent. The following passages do not represent radical new departures for black leaders, but they differ from their predecessors in the extent of their dissemination and in the fact that many of their hearers were willing to act upon them.

Jim Brown, famous ex-fullback for the Cleveland Browns and later a movie star, recalled a nearly disastrous encounter with racial violence which occurred while he was an All-American football player at Syracuse University. [From "*Playboy* Interview: Jim Brown" (*Playboy* magazine, February 1968); reprinted by permission of *Playboy* magazine.]

Playboy: Have you encountered any other kind of overt discrimination since you became well known?

Brown: Are you kidding? I don't even like to think about it. But I'll give you just one example. There was nothing really uncommon about the incident itself in the average Negro's experience, particularly in the South. But it had me choked up and bitter for a long time after it happened. It was in 1957 and I was in Army training down in Alabama. Three buddies of mine and I were in my convertible, with the top down, driving to Tuskegee. We had just gone through this little town, enjoying ourselves, when all of a sudden this police car roared up behind and barreled past us, cut us off and stopped; and, baby, I'm looking at this cop getting out with a drawn gun. "Get out, niggers!" We got out. "What are you making dust all over white people for?" Just about then, another car pulled up and stopped and another white guy got out. The cop was saying, "You hear me, nigger?" Well, my emotions were such that I hardly trusted myself to speak. "I don't know what a nigger is!" I said. Then he jammed the pistol right in my stomach. "Nigger, don't you know how to talk to white folks?" One of the guys with me said, "He's not from down here, he's from up North." The cop said, "Nigger, I don't care where you're from. I'll blow you apart! Where did you get this car, anyway?" I said, "It was given to me." He said, "*Given* to you! Who gave you a *car?*" I said, "It was given to me at school." "*What* school?" I said, "Syracuse University." Just about then, the other white man came over closer and he said, "That's right. I recognize this boy. He plays football up there." That was my reprieve. The cop took the gun out of my belly and said, "I'm going to let you go, but you better drive slow and you better learn how to act down here, nigger!" So we got back in the car and drove on. I don't know why I even told you that; it's not good to dredge that stuff up in your mind again. But you see, you don't forget a thing like that, not if somebody handed you every trophy in football and 15 Academy Awards. That's why a black man, if he's got any sense at all, will never get swept away with special treatment if he happens to be famous, because he knows that the minute he isn't where somebody *recognizes* who he is, then he's just another *nigger*. That's what the Negro struggle is all about; that's why we black people have to keep fighting for freedom in this country. We demand only to live—and let live—like any ordinary American. We don't want to have to be somebody *special* to be treated with respect. I can't understand why white people find it so hard to understand that.

Malcolm X, a ghetto hustler before his conversion to the black Nation of Islam, provided charismatic leadership for masses of blacks whose feelings and aspirations he articulated. He preached a gospel of self-discovery, brotherhood, courage, and racial pride. [Malcolm X speech to rally supporting the Mississippi Freedom Democratic Party, in Harlem, December 20, 1964. From *Macolm X Speaks* (New York: Grove Press, 1965), pp. 107–8. Reprinted by permission of Merit Publishers.]

When I was in Africa, I noticed some of the Africans got their freedom faster than others. Some areas of the African continent became independent faster than other areas. I noticed that in the areas where independence had been gotten, someone got angry. And in the areas where independence had not been achieved yet, no one was angry. They were sad—they'd sit around and talk about their plight, but they weren't mad. And usually, when people are sad, they don't do anything. They just cry over their condition.

But when they get angry, they bring about a change. When they get angry, they aren't interested in logic, they aren't interested in odds, they aren't interested in consequences. When they get angry, they realize the condition that they're in—that their suffering is unjust, immoral, illegal, and that anything they do to correct it or eliminate it, they're justified. When you and I develop that type of anger and speak in that voice, then we'll get some kind of respect and recognition, and some changes from these people who have been promising us falsely already for far too long.

. . . I put the blame on that man who gave the orders. And when you and I begin to look at him and see the language he speaks, the language of a brute, the language of someone who has no sense of morality, who absolutely ignores law—when you and I learn how to speak his language, then we can communicate. But we will never communicate talking one language while he's talking another language. He's talking the language of violence while you and I are running around with this little chicken-picking type of language—and think that he's going to understand.

Let's learn his language. If his language is with a shotgun, get a shotgun. Yes, I said if he only understands the language of a rifle, get a rifle. If he only understands the language of a rope, get a rope. But don't waste time talking the wrong language to a man if you want to really communicate with him. Speak his language—there's nothing wrong with that. If something was wrong with that language, the federal government would have stopped the cracker from speaking it to you and me.

Frantz Fanon, a French African writing of African anti-colonialism, articulated the positive benefits of revolutionary violence. [Frantz Fanon, *The Wretched of the Earth*, trans. from the French by Constance Farrington (New York: Grove Press, Inc., 1968), pp. 37, 43, 83–84, 93, 94. Reprinted by permission of Grove Press, Inc.]

The naked truth of decolonization evokes for us the searing bullets and bloodstained knives which emanate from it. For if the last shall be first, this will only come to pass after a murderous and decisive struggle between the two protagonists. That affirmed intention to place the last at the head of things, and to make them climb at a pace (too quickly, some say) the well-known steps which characterize an organized society, can only triumph if we use all means to turn the scale, including, of course, that of violence.

You do not turn any society, however primitive it may be, upside down with such a program if you have not decided from the very beginning, that is to say from the actual formulation of that program, to overcome all the obstacles that you will come across in so doing. The native who decides to put the program into practice, and to become its moving force, is ready for violence at all times. From birth it is clear to him that this narrow world, strewn with prohibitions, can only be called in question by absolute violence.

*   *   *

. . . The violence with which the supremacy of white values is affirmed and the aggressiveness which had permeated the victory of these values over the ways of life and of thought of the native mean that, in revenge, the native laughs in mockery when Western values are mentioned in front of him. In the colonial context the settler only ends his work of breaking in the native when the latter admits loudly and intelligibly the supremacy of the white man's values. In the period of decolonization, the colonized masses mock at these very values, insult them, and vomit them up.

*   *   *

The existence of an armed struggle shows that the people are decided to trust to violent methods only. He of whom *they* have never stopped saying that the only language he understands is that of force, decides to give utterance by force. In fact, as always, the settler has shown him the way he should take if he is to become free. The argument the native chooses has been furnished by the settler, and by an ironic turning of the tables it is the native who now affirms that the colonialist understands nothing but force. The colonial regime owes its legitimacy to force and at no time tries to hide this aspect of things.

*   *   *

But it so happens that for the colonized people this violence, because it constitutes their only work, invests their characters with positive and creative qualities. The practice of violence binds them together as a whole, since each individual forms a violent link in the great chain, a part of the great organism of violence which has surged upward in reaction to the settler's violence in the beginning. The groups recognize each other and the future nation is already indivisible. The armed struggle mobilizes the people; that is to say, it throws them in one way and in one direction.

*   *   *

At the levels of individuals, violence is a cleansing force. It frees the native from his inferiority complex and from his despair and inaction; it makes him fearless and restores his self-respect.

☞ 4 ☜

THE POWDER KEG

Riots do not just happen. They are not totally aberrant outbursts that originate with individual persons or isolated incidents, just as explosions do not result from matches alone. Each city in which a riot has erupted has been a powder keg.

The basic ingredients of such a powder keg are the antagonistic white and black roles in the American caste system and the mutual acceptance of violence as a means of defending or attacking that system. Constant interracial friction produces a certain amount of powder. In the city, where population and environment are perpetually in motion, the points of friction are greatest and this powder accumulates rapidly. Residential invasion was a highly visible cause of friction in both the Chicago (1919) and Detroit (1943) riots; in both cases, invasion of recreational facilities supplied the immediate context in which the spark was struck. As blacks move to cities, both natural selection and formal and informal segregation assign them to restricted residential areas. Living conditions, including the sense of total confinement, in these ghettos spawn a variety of ghetto pathologies and a reservoir of resentment. At the same time, the massing of blacks in a ghetto provides possibilities for black unity, self-development, indigenous leaders, and group identification. It also diminishes personal interracial contact (as compared with slavery or a rural setting), thus permitting blacks greater freedom from white surveillance. This in turn threatens the maintenance of caste control: the many "niggertowns" have bothered whites, who are suspicious of what goes on in them and are tempted to raid and break them up.

This characteristic of urban life is related to the whole range of consequences of the anonymity and impersonality of the city. When whites riot, they can abuse any black who happens along since they likely do not know him and "they all look alike to me." This indiscriminate assaulting distinguishes a riot from a lynching, for the latter has a definite (innocent or guilty) object of attack. Conversely, when blacks strike out against their environments they can attack "the Man." At the same time that the predominance of secondary and tertiary relationships makes it easier for both white and black to participate in riots, they force a greater reliance on external devices of social control. In slavery days this often meant a slaveowner shifted the task of administering physical punishment onto a municipal magistrate. Since then, because upholding the caste system is part of social control, the law enforcement official spends much of his time acting out the ritual (for benefit of black and white) of forcefully subjecting the black to white domination.

Both despite and because of his separation, city living supplies the black with continuing evidence of discrimination. He perceives residential segregation, employment discrimination, and income differentials. In a Southern city he daily rode a jim crow streetcar and looked for "colored only" signs; in Northern cities he sits where he pleases, but notes white disapproval. And seldom can he regard a policeman as his friend and protector. The conditions of urban living have intensified the black man's sense of estrangement from the total society.

Immediate historical settings which have prepared the powder keg include war, political strife, labor disturbances, and lax law enforcement. A war or postwar setting figured in riots in New York (1863), Memphis (1866), New Orleans (1866), Houston and East St. Louis (1917), Chicago and Washington (1919), Detroit and Harlem (1943), and Los Angeles, Cleveland, Newark, Detroit, Washington, and others (1960s). Common to all have been tremendous population shifts, occupational upgrading for blacks, an intensification of violence (and its apparent toleration by the public), and military service attended by enhanced pride and intensified bitterness by blacks. In Memphis (1866) and Houston (1917) sporadic clashes between black troops and white law enforcement officers heightened tensions.

Labor strife has provided another potentially explosive context. Besides the job competition common to wartime riots, there have been strikes and conflicts over labor unionization. In East St. Louis manufacturers imported black laborers from the South, thereby helping to defeat a strike for union recognition. In Memphis (1968) a strike by garbage collectors served as a background for disturbances.

Crusades against vice and lax law enforcement in Atlanta (1906) and Tulsa (1921) and demoralized municipal authorities in Memphis (1866), Springfield, Ill. (1908), East St. Louis (1917), Chicago (1919), and Newark (1967) added to the explosive mixture. Political contests involving blatant appeals to prejudice figured in Atlanta (1906 and 1966), and in Memphis and New Orleans (1866). All these ingredients contributed to a powder keg awaiting an incident to ignite an explosion.

Urban Crisis in the 1960s

On July 29, 1967, President Lyndon B. Johnson established a National Advisory Commission on Civil Disorders and charged it to examine thoroughly the origins, basic causes, and factors leading up to the outbreaks during that summer, and to suggest remedies that might control and avert future riots. The Kerner Commission (so-called after Governor Otto Kerner of Illinois, its chairman) produced a report which stirred up substantial controversy. For blacks, its conclusions were hardly startling; but many whites, few of whom had actually read it, were incensed. Eschewing preoccupation with agitators, conspiracies, and defense of the status quo, it forthrightly proclaimed that the cause of civil disorder was historical white racism. The Kerner Report provides a standard of thorough and honest investigation; neither vindictive nor maudlin, it absolved neither black nor white and assigned responsibility to society at large, both past and present. [From *Report of the National Advisory Commission on Civil Disorders* (Washington, 1968), pp. 91–93. (Hereafter called the Kerner Report.)]

We have seen what happened. Why did it happen?

In addressing this question we shift our focus from the local to the national scene, from the particular events of the summer of 1967 to the factors within the society at large that created a mood for violence among so many urban Negroes.

The record before this Commission reveals that the causes of recent racial disorders are imbedded in a massive tangle of issues and circumstances—social, economic, political, and psychological—which arise out of the historical pattern of Negro-white relations in America.

These factors are both complex and interacting; they vary significantly in their effect from city to city and from year to year; and the consequences of one disorder, generating new grievances and new demands, become the causes of the next. It is this which creates the "thicket of tension, conflicting evidence and extreme opinions" cited by the President.

Despite these complexities, certain fundamental matters are clear. Of these, the most fundamental is the racial attitude and behavior of white Americans toward black Americans. Race prejudice has shaped our history decisively in the past; it now threatens to do so again. White racism is essentially responsible for the explosive mixture which has been accumulating in our cities since the end of World War II. At the base of this mixture are three of the most bitter fruits of white racial attitudes:

Pervasive discrimination and segregation. The first is surely the continuing exclusion of great numbers of Negroes from the benefits of economic progress through discrimination in employment and education and their enforced confinement in segregated housing and schools. The corrosive and degrading effects of this condition and the attitudes that underlie it are the source of the deepest bitterness and lie at the center of the problem of racial disorder.

Black migration and white exodus. The second is the massive and growing concentration of impoverished Negroes in our major cities resulting from Negro migration from the rural South, rapid population growth, and the continuing movement of the white middle-class to the suburbs. The consequence is a greatly increased burden on the already depleted resources of cities, creating a growing crisis of deteriorating facilities and services and unmet human needs.

Black ghettos. Third, in the teeming racial ghettos, segregation and poverty have intersected to destroy opportunity and hope and to enforce failure. The ghettos too often mean men and women without jobs, families without men, and schools where children are processed instead of educated, until they return to the street—to crime, to narcotics, to dependency on welfare, and to bitterness and resentment against society in general and white society in particular.

These three forces have converged on the inner city in recent years and on the people who inhabit it. At the same time, most whites and many Negroes outside the ghetto have prospered to a degree unparalleled in the history of civilization. Through television—the universal appliance in the ghetto—and the other media of mass communications, this affluence has been endlessly flaunted before the eyes of the Negro poor and the jobless ghetto youth.

As Americans, most Negro citizens carry within themselves two basic aspirations of our society. They seek to share in both the material resources of our system and its intangible benefits—dignity, respect, and acceptance. Outside the ghetto many have succeeded in achieving a decent standard of life, and in developing the inner resources which give life meaning and direction. Within the ghetto, however, it is rare that either aspiration is achieved.

Yet these facts alone—fundamental as they are—cannot be said to have caused the disorders. Other and more immediate factors help explain why these events happened now.

Recently, three powerful ingredients have begun to catalyze the mixture.

Frustrated hopes. The expectations aroused by the great judicial and legislative victories of the civil rights movement have led to frustration, hostility, and cynicism in the face of the persistent gap between promise and fulfillment. The dramatic struggle for equal rights in the South has sensitized northern Negroes to the economic inequalities reflected in the deprivations of ghetto life.

Legitimation of violence. A climate that tends toward the approval and encouragement of violence as a form of protest has been created by white terrorism directed against nonviolent protest, including instances of abuse and even murder of some civil rights workers in the South, by the open defiance of law and Federal authority by state and local officials resisting desegregation, and by some protest groups engaging in civil disobedience who turn their backs on nonviolence, go beyond the constitutionally protected rights of petition and free assembly, and resort to violence to attempt to compel alteration of laws and policies with which they disagree. This condition has been reinforced by a general erosion of respect for authority in American society and reduced effectiveness of social standards and community restraints on violence and crime. This in turn has largely resulted from rapid urbanization and the dramatic reduction in the average age of the total population.

Powerlessness. Finally, many Negroes have come to believe that they are being exploited politically and economically by the white "power structure." Negroes, like people in poverty everywhere, in fact lack the channels of communication, influence, and appeal that traditionally have been available to ethnic minorities within the city and which enabled them—unburdened by color—to scale the walls of the white ghettos in an earlier era. The frustrations of powerlessness have led some to the conviction that there is no effective alternative to violence as a means of expression and redress, as a way of "moving the system." More generally, the result is alienation and hostility toward the institutions of law and government and the white society which controls them. This is reflected in the reach toward racial consciousness and solidarity reflected in the slogan "Black Power."

These facts have combined to inspire a new mood among Negroes, particularly among the young. Self-esteem and enhanced racial pride are replacing apathy and submission to "the system." Moreover, Negro youth, who make up over half of the ghetto population, share the growing sense of alienation felt by many white youth in our country. Thus, their role in recent civil disorders reflects not only a shared sense of deprivation and victimization by white society but also the rising incidence of disruptive conduct by a segment of American youth throughout the society.

Incitement and encouragement of violence. These conditions have created a volatile mixture of attitudes and beliefs which needs only a spark to ignite mass violence. Strident appeals to violence, first heard from white racists, were echoed and reinforced last summer in the inflammatory rhetoric of black racists and militants. Throughout the year, extremists crisscrossed the country preaching a doctrine of black power and violence. Their rhetoric was widely reported in the mass media; it was echoed by local "militants" and organizations; it became the ugly background noise of the violent summer.

We cannot measure with any precision the influence of these organizations and individuals in the ghetto, but we think it clear that the intolerable and unconscionable encouragement of violence heightened tensions, created a mood of acceptance and an expectation of violence, and thus contributed to the eruption of the disorders last summer.

The Police. It is the convergence of all these factors that makes the role of the police so difficult and so significant. Almost invariably the incident that ignites disorder arises from police action. Harlem, Watts, Newark and Detroit—all the major outbursts of recent years—were precipitated by routine arrests of Negroes for minor offenses by white police.

But the police are not merely the spark. In discharge of their obligation to maintain order and insure public safety in the disruptive conditions of ghetto life, they are inevitably involved in sharper and more frequent conflicts with ghetto residents than with the residents of other areas. Thus, to many Negroes, police have come to symbolize white power, white racism, and white repression. And the fact is that many police do reflect and express these white attitudes. The atmosphere of hostility and cynicism is reinforced by a widespread perception among Negroes of the existence of police brutality and corruption, and of a "double standard" of justice and protection—one for Negroes and one for whites.

The 1965 California Governor's Commission on the Los Angeles Riots, headed by former CIA head John A. McCone, while not so comprehensive as the later Kerner Report, did make some observations about the underlying conditions—the "dull, devastating spiral of failure" it called them—in Los Angeles' Watts ghetto. [From *Violence in the City—An End or a Beginning?* A Report by the Governor's Commission on the Los Angeles Riots (hereafter called the McCone Report). December 2, 1965, pp. 81–82.]

The study of the Los Angeles riots which we have now completed brought us face to face with the deepening problems that confront America. They are the problems of transition created by three decades of change during which the historical pattern of urban and rural life

—which for decades before existed side by side, each complementing and supporting the other—has been violently and irreversibly altered. Modern methods and mechanization of the farm have dramatically, and, in some regards, sadly reduced the need for the farm hand. With this, a drift to the city was the inevitable and necessary result. With respect to the Negro, the drift was first to the urban centers of the South and then, because scanty means of livelihood existed there, on northward and westward to the larger metropolitan centers. It was not the Negro alone who drifted; a substantial part of the entire farm labor force, white and Negro alike, was forced to move and did.

World War II and, to a lesser extent, the Korean War of the early '50's, tended to accelerate the movement, particularly the drift of the Negro from the south to the north. Because job opportunities existed in the war plants located in our cities, the deep and provocative problem created by the movement was not at first appreciated by society. Since then, caught up in almost a decade of struggle with civil rights and its related problems, most of America focused its attention upon the problem of the South—and only a few turned their attention and thoughts to the explosive situation of our cities.

But the conditions of life in the urban north and west were sadly disappointing to the rural newcomer, particularly the Negro. Totally untrained, he was qualified only for jobs calling for the lesser skills and these he secured and held onto with great difficulty. Even the jobs he found in the city soon began to disappear as the mechanization of industry took over, as it has since the war, and wiped out one task after another—the only tasks the untrained Negro was equipped to fill.

Hence, equality of opportunity, a privilege he sought and expected, proved more of an illusion than a fact. The Negro found that he entered the competitive life of the city with very real handicaps: he lacked education, training, and experience, and his handicaps were aggravated by racial barriers which were more traditional than legal. He found himself, for reasons for which he had no responsibility and over which he had no control, in a situation in which providing a livelihood for himself and his family was most difficult and at times desperate. Thus, with the passage of time, altogether too often the rural Negro who has come to the city sinks into despair. And many of the younger generation, coming on in great numbers, inherit this feeling but seek release, not in apathy, but in ways which, if allowed to run unchecked, offer nothing but tragedy to America.

[From Carey McWilliams, "Watts: The Forgotten Slum," editorial in *The Nation*, August 30, 1965. Selections from *The Nation* are reprinted by permission of the publisher.]

Thirty-one dead, over 700 injured, 2,200 under arrest, 1,000 fires, property damage of $200 million—such is the preliminary toll for the long weekend of rioting in the Watts area of Los Angeles. A feverish search for scapegoats is now under way and will no doubt continue through the 1966 gubernatorial campaign. High on the scapegoat list is the self-righteous Chief of Police who dismisses as a "canard" the charge that the Los Angeles police could ever be guilty of brutality; apparently Chief Parker doesn't watch television. Then there is Sam Yorty, the agile Mayor, playing political tricks as always; warned of the possibility of riots, he did nothing. The list is long and includes The Heat—a favorite scapegoat in all race-riot investigations—and Social Conditions. Here Watts qualifies on all counts: dropouts, delinquency, disease and dependency. But none of these social factors alone or in combination necessarily "cause" race riots; actually it is when conditions seem to be improving that the riots usually explode. Predictably the forthcoming investigation ordered by Governor Brown will stress the same tiresome cliches: police brutality, inadequate leadership, The Heat, slum conditions. All the while the truth about Watts is right there in front of people, in plain boldface type, for all to read; so simple that it is incredible. The hatred and violence of race riots is triggered by contempt, and of all forms of contempt the most intolerable is nonrecognition, the general unawareness that a minority is festering in squalor. Until the riots began, Watts had simply been forgotten by the encompassing "white" community.

Housing and Occupational Invasion

The Chicago Commission on Race Relations combined public and private resources to examine the broad question of Negro conditions in Chicago following the riot there in 1919. Among its exhaustive findings were evidences of organized discrimination in real estate selling. [From Chicago Commission on Race Relations, *The Negro in Chicago* (Chicago: University of Chicago Press, 1922), pp. 116–20.]

"Contested neighborhoods."—The contested neighborhoods are by far the most important among the types of non-adjusted neighborhoods, both because of the actual presence in them of varying numbers of Negroes and their bearing on the future relations of the races. The efforts in such neighborhoods to keep out Negroes involve stimulation of anti-Negro sentiment and organization of property owners,

and the campaign against the presence of Negroes as neighbors develops into a campaign against Negroes. Negroes in turn resent both the propaganda statements and the organized efforts. A continuous struggle, marked by bombings, foreclosures of mortgages, and court disputes, is the result.

The most conspicuous type of a "contested neighborhood" is that known as Kenwood and Hyde Park. In this general neighborhood, from Thirty-ninth to Fifty-ninth streets and from State Street to Lake Michigan, hostility toward Negroes has been plainly and even forcibly expressed through organized efforts to oust them and prevent their further encroachment. The situation is peculiar. This is the part of the old South Side in which most of the Negro population of Chicago has settled. The so-called "Black Belt" has been overcrowded for years. Old and deteriorated housing and its insufficiency have been steadily driving Negroes out of it in search of other homes.

*   *   *

Organization of sentiment: It does not appear that the residents of this neighborhood rose spontaneously to oppose the coming in of Negroes. If this had been the case, the first Negroes moving into the district in 1917 would have felt the opposition. The sudden interest in race occupancy was based upon the alleged depreciation of property by Negroes. With this emphasized, it was not difficult to rally opposition to Negroes as a definite menace. The real estate men gave the alarm, alleging a shrinkage in property values. The effort through the Hyde Park and Kenwood Association was intended to stop the influx and thereby the depreciation. Meetings were held, a newspaper was published, and literature was distributed. Racial antagonism was strong in the speeches at these meetings and in the newspapers. The meeting which probably marked the first focusing of attention on the Kenwood and Hyde Park districts was held May 5, 1919, when the sentiment was expressed that Negro invasion of the district was the worst calamity that had struck the city since the Great Fire. A prominent white real estate man said: "Property owners should be notified to stand together block by block and prevent such invasion."

*   *   *

Other remarks of speakers at these meetings were:

The depreciation of our property in this district has been two hundred and fifty millions since the invasion. If someone told you that there was to be an invasion that would injure your homes to that extent, wouldn't you rise up as one man and one woman, and say as General Foch said: "They shall not pass"?

There isn't an insurance company in America that will turn around and try to buck our organization when we as one man give them to understand that it is dangerous to insure some people.

Why I remember fifteen or twenty years ago that the district down here at Wabash Avenue and Calumet was one of the most beautiful and highest-class neighborhoods of this great city. Go down there to-day and see the ramshackle broken-down and tumble-down district. That is the result of the new menace that is threatening this great Hyde Park district. And then tell me whether there are or not enough red-blooded, patriotic, loyal, courageous citizens of Hyde Park to save this glorious district from the menace which has brought so much pain and so much disaster to the district to the south of us.

You cannot mix oil and water. You cannot assimilate races of a different color as neighbors along social lines. Remember this: That order is heaven's first law.

Walter White, secretary of the NAACP, devoted much of the Association's report on the causes of the riot in Detroit in 1943 to the massive influx of Southern migrants, black and white, and the overt hostility whites directed against the upgrading of blacks in Detroit's war-time industries. [From Walter White, "What Caused the Detroit Riots?," in *The Crisis* (1943), pp. 5–7. Selections from *The Crisis* are reprinted by permission of the Crisis Publishing Company.]

According to the War Manpower Commission, approximately 500,-000 immigrants moved to Detroit between June, 1940, and June, 1943. Because of discrimination against employment of Negroes in industry, the overwhelming majority—between 40,000 and 50,000—of the approximately 50,000 Negroes who went to Detroit in this three-year period moved there during the fifteen months prior to the race riot of June, 1943. According to Governor Harry S. Kelly, of Michigan, a total of 345,000 persons moved into Detroit during that same fifteen-month period. There was comparatively little out-migration as industry called for more and more workers in one of the tightest labor markets in the United States. The War Manpower Commission failed almost completely to enforce its edict that no in-migration be permitted into any industrial area until all available local labor was utilized. Thus a huge reservoir of Negro labor existed in Detroit, crowded into highly-congested slum areas. But they did have housing of a sort and this labor was already in Detroit. The coming of white workers recruited chiefly in the South not only gravely complicated the housing, transportation, educational and recreation facilities of Detroit, but they brought with them the traditional prejudices of Mississippi, Arkansas, Louisiana, and other Deep South states against the Negro.

✳   ✳   ✳

For years preceding the riot, there had been mob attacks dating back as far as the famous Sweet case in 1925 upon the homes of Negroes. In some instances there had been police connivance in these attacks. In practically no cases had there been arrests of whites who had stoned or bombed the homes of Negroes. During July, 1941, there had been an epidemic of riots allegedly by Polish youths which had terrorized colored residents in Detroit, Hamtramck and other sections in and about Detroit. Homes of Negroes on Horton, Chippewa, West Grand Boulevard and other streets close to but outside of the so-called Negro areas were attacked by mobs with no police interference.

* * *

Early in June, 1943, 25,000 employes of the Packard Plant, which was making Rolls-Royce engines for American bombers and marine engines for the famous PT boats, ceased work in protest against the upgrading of three Negroes. Subsequent investigation indicated that only a relatively small percentage of the Packard workers actually wanted to go on strike. The UAW-CIO bitterly fought the strike. But a handful of agitators charged by R. J. Thomas, president of the UAW-CIO, with being members of the Ku Klux Klan, had whipped up sentiment particularly among the Southern whites employed by Packard against the promotion of Negro workers. During the short-lived strike, a thick Southern voice outside the plant harangued a crowd shouting, "I'd rather see Hitler and Hirohito win than work beside a nigger on the assembly line." The strike was broken by the resolute attitude of the union and of Col. George E. Strong of the United States Aircraft procurement Division, who refused to yield to the demand that the three Negroes be down-graded. Certain officials of the Packard Company were clearly responsible in part for the strike. C. E. Weiss, Personnel Manager, George Schwartz, General Foreman, and Robert Watts of the Personnel Division, urged the strikers to hold out in their demand that Negroes not be hired or upgraded. Weiss is alleged to have told the men that they did not have to work beside Negroes. At the time this report is written, Weiss, Schwartz, and Watts are still employed by the Packard Motor Car Company. The racial hatred created, released, and crystallized by the Packard strike played a considerable role in the race riot which was soon to follow. It also was the culmination of a long and bitter fight to prevent the employment of Negroes in wartime industry. There had been innumerable instances, unpublicized, in the Detroit area of work stoppages and slow downs by white workers, chiefly from the South, and of Polish and Italian extraction. Trivial reasons for these stoppages had been given by the workers when in reality they were in protest against employment or promotion of Negroes. A vast number of man hours and of production had been irretrievably lost through these stoppages.

A committee of United States Congressmen reported on the housing and occupational friction preceding the bloody massacre at East St. Louis in 1917. [From *East St. Louis Riots* (House Document 1231, 65th Congress, 2nd Session), printed in *Congressional Record*, Vol. 56, Pt. 9 (65th Cong., 2nd Sess., July 6, 1918), p. 8826.]

The natural racial aversion, which finds expression in mob violence in the North as in the South, was augmented in East St. Louis by hundreds of petty conflicts between the whites and the blacks. During the year 1917 between 10,000 and 12,000 negroes came from the Southern States to seek work at promised high wages in the industries of St. Clair County. They swarmed into the railroad stations on every train, to be met by their friends who formed reception committees and welcomed them to the financial, political and social liberty which they had been led to believe Illinois guaranteed. They seldom had more than enough money to exactly defray their transportation, and they arrived dirty and hungry. They stood around the street corners in homesick huddles, seeking shelter and hunting work.

How to deal with them soon became a municipal problem. Morning found them gathered at the gates of the manufactories, where often they were chosen in preference to the white men who also sought employment. But as rapidly as employment was found for those already there fresh swarms arrived from the South, until the great number without employment menaced the prosperity and safety of the community.

The Aluminum Ore Co. brought hundreds and hundreds of them to the city as strike breakers, to defeat organized labor, a precedent which aroused intense hatred and antagonism and caused countless tragedies as its aftermath. The feeling of resentment grew with each succeeding day. White men walked the streets in idleness, their families suffering for food and warmth and clothes, while their places as laborers were taken by strange negroes who were compelled to live in hovels and who were used to keep down wages.

It was proven conclusively that the various industries in St. Clair County were directly responsible for the importation of these negroes from the South. Advertisements were printed in various Southern newspapers urging the negroes to come to East St. Louis and promising them big wages. In many instances agents were sent through the South to urge the negroes to abandon profitable employment there and come to East St. Louis, where work was said to be plentiful and wages high.

Government and Politics

Urbanites tend to look toward their elected officials to solve or at least ameliorate some of the problems occasioned by rapid urban growth. Thus governmental incapacity and political strife may contribute substantially to a city's accumulation of powder.

The Kerner Commission found that Newark in 1967 was a city in the throes of acute center decay and governmental paralysis. [From Kerner Report, pp. 30–31.]

Founded in 1666, the city, part of the Greater New York City port complex, rises from the salt marshes of the Passaic River. Although in 1967 Newark's population of 400,000 still ranked it thirtieth among American municipalities, for the past 20 years the white middle class had been deserting the city for the suburbs.

In the late 1950's the desertions had become a rout. Between 1960 and 1967, the city lost a net total of more than 70,000 white residents. Replacing them in vast areas of dilapidated housing where living conditions, according to a prominent member of the County Bar Association, were so bad that "people would be kinder to their pets," were Negro migrants, Cubans and Puerto Ricans. In 6 years the city switched from 65 per cent white to 52 per cent Negro and 10 per cent Puerto Rican and Cuban.

The white population, nevertheless, retained political control of the city. On both the city council and the board of education seven of nine members were white. On other key boards the disparity was equal or greater. In the central ward, where the medical college controversy raged, the Negro constituents and their white councilman found themselves on opposite sides of almost every crucial issue.

The municipal administration lacked the ability to respond quickly enough to navigate the swiftly changing currents. Even had it had great astuteness, it would have lacked the financial resources to affect significantly the course of events.

In 1962, seven-term Congressman Hugh Addonizio had forged an Italian-Negro coalition to overthrow long-time Irish control of the City Hall. A liberal in Congress, Addonizio, when he became mayor, had opened his door to all people. Negroes, who had been excluded from the previous administration, were brought into the government. The police department was integrated.

Nevertheless, progress was slow. As the Negro population increased, more and more of the politically oriented found the progress inadequate.

The Negro-Italian coalition began to develop strains over the issue of the police. The police were largely Italian, the persons they arrested were largely Negro. Community leaders agreed that, as in many police forces, there was a small minority of officers who abused their responsibility. This gave credibility to the cries of "Brutality!" voiced periodically by ghetto Negroes.

*   *   *

The city had already reached its legal bonding limit, yet expenditures continued to outstrip income. Health and welfare costs, per capita, were 20 times as great as for some of the surrounding communities. Cramped by its small land area of 23.6 square miles—one-third of which was taken up by Newark Airport and unusable marshland—and surrounded by independent jurisdictions, the city had nowhere to expand.

Taxable property was contracting as land, cleared for urban renewal, lay fallow year after year. Property taxes had been increased, perhaps, to the point of diminishing return. By the fall of 1967 they were to reach $661.70 on a $10,000 house—double that of suburban communities. As a result, people were refusing either to own or to renovate property in the city. Seventy-four per cent of white and 87 per cent of Negro families lived in rental housing. Whoever was able to move to the suburbs, moved. Many of these persons, as downtown areas were cleared and new office buildings were constructed, continued to work in the city. Among them were a large proportion of the people from whom a city normally draws its civic leaders, but who, after moving out, tended to cease involving themselves in the community's problems.

During the daytime Newark more than doubled its population—and was, therefore, forced to provide services for a large number of people who contributed nothing in property taxes. The city's per capita outlay for police, fire protection, and other municipal services continued to increase. By 1967 it was twice that of the surrounding area.

Consequently, there was less money to spend on education. Newark's per capita outlay on schools was considerably less than that of surrounding communities. Yet within the city's school system were 78,-000 children, 14,000 more than 10 years earlier.

Twenty thousand pupils were on double sessions. The drop-out rate was estimated to be as high as 33 per cent. Of 13,600 Negroes between the ages of 16 and 19, more than 6,000 were not in school. In 1960 over half of the adult Negro population had less than an eighth grade education.

The typical ghetto cycle of high unemployment, family breakup, and crime was present in all its elements. Approximately 12 per cent of Negroes were without jobs. An estimated 40 per cent of Negro children lived in broken homes. Although Newark maintained proportionately the largest police force of any major city, its crime rate was among the highest in the nation. In narcotics violations it ranked fifth nationally. Almost 80 per cent of the crimes were committed within 2 miles of the core of the city, where the Central Ward is located. A majority of the criminals were Negro. Most of the victims, likewise, were Negro. The Mafia was reputed to control much of the organized crime.

The politics of racism added substantially to the explosive mixture building up in Atlanta in 1906. Georgia experienced a vituperative campaign for the Democratic gubernatorial nomination which began in mid-1905 and lasted until Hoke Smith received the nomination in September, 1906. The contest finally came to center on the question of Negro disfranchisement, and the entire campaign constituted a blatant emotional appeal to white prejudice. [From the nominating speech, delivered by Mr. James L. Anderson before the Democratic convention of Georgia, presenting Hoke Smith as the gubernatorial candidate, September 4, 1906. Printed in the *Atlanta Constitution*, September 5, 1906.]

Mr. Chairman, with sincere conviction, I insist that the crime committed against us by the passage of the fifteenth amendment to the constitution of the United States is responsible for the stench of negro insolence, which has blighted this glorious southland, and soiled southern womanhood these forty years; that political equality, and the thwarted hope of social equality, have made of the old-time humble negro a demon, with a heart full of hatred toward the white man. Mr. Smith's victory means an end of this—it means that the south, under his leadership, will appeal to and convert our brothers of the north and west. The fifteenth amendment will ultimately be repealed, and we shall realize the glorious noonday of a united white people, in absolute control of the white man's country. Yes, Mr. Chairman, our northern brothers must, and will, undo and nullify the horrible crime which they perpetrated against us in the heat of passion and the lust of blood, at the close of the civil war. The white man, even if unlettered, is descended of a long line of noble ancestors—to whom is due this present high order of civilization; the white man through centuries of toil and suffering, and through blood, snatched this beautiful land from the savage, and made a wilderness to blossom; it is his heritage; in its government and control does he need the aid of a semi-barbarian, only recently emerged from the jungles of Africa? So have our friends of the north endeavored to teach us through the fifteenth amendment. This doctrine, if carried to its proper conclusion, means that the negro is the equal of the white man, and justifies Booker Washington at Roosevelt's lunch table or leading Wannamaker's daughter to dinner.

*   *   *

My friends, let us all press forward—as brothers running together—under the leadership of this strong man, whom God has sent to us in a time of great need; and let us establish in Georgia, in the south—yes, in America, the doctrine of everlasting white supremacy. Let color be the line of demarcation. Put it squarely here. The most illiterate white man has, through inheritance, noble conceptions, and hears heavenly music, which neither education or association can make perceptible to the negro, in whose soul the darkness of savagery is just beginning to fade into twilight.

No, the negro for ages—perhaps always—must be the servant of the white man; he has no other place in a white man's country. He shall not aspire to equality with the white man. We must nullify—yes, repeal—this odious fifteenth amendment; else, my friends—miserable thought—the educated negro is justified in his claim of social equality with the white man, and in his attentions to the white man's daughter.

*   *   *

I present Mr. Smith as the chaiman [sic] of the white people of Georgia, and of the south. His election will mean the dawn of a new and glorious day.

Such campaigns as Hoke Smith's in 1906 were as disruptive in the long as in the short run. Traditionally excluded from voting, blacks were compelled to look outside the orderly political process for redress of public grievances. The Kerner Commission found political powerlessness to be a common condition in cities where riots had occurred in 1967. [From the Kerner Report, "Tampa," p. 23, and "Cincinnati," p. 26.]

Although officials prided themselves on supposedly good race relations and relative acceptance by whites of integration of schools and facilities, Negroes, composing almost 20 per cent of the population, had had no one of their own race to represent them in positions of policy or power, nor to appeal to for redress of grievances.

There was no Negro on the city council; none on the school board; none in the fire department; none of high rank on the police force. Six of every 10 houses inhabited by Negroes were unsound. Many were shacks with broken window panes, gas leads, and rat holes in the walls. Rents averaged $50 to $60 a month. Such recreational facilities as did exist lacked equipment and supervisors. Young toughs intimidated the children who tried to use them.

The majority of Negro children never reached the eighth grade. In the high schools, only 3 to 4 per cent of Negro seniors attained the minimum passing score on the State's college entrance examination, one-tenth the percentage of white students.

* * *

. . . Without the city's realizing what was occurring, over the years protest through political and non-violent channels had become increasingly difficult for Negroes. To young, militant Negroes, especially, such protest appeared to have become almost futile.

Although the city's Negro population had been rising swiftly—in 1967, 135,000 out of the city's 500,000 residents were Negroes—there was only one Negro on the city council. In the 1950's with a far smaller Negro population, there had been two. Negroes attributed this to dilution of the Negro vote through abolition of the proportional representation system of electing the nine councilmen.

Although, by 1967, 40 per cent of the schoolchildren were Negro, there was only one Negro on the board of education. Of more than 80 members of various city commissions, only three or four were Negro.

Attitudes in Wartime

This editorial in Detroit's largest black newspaper called its readers' attention to a congeries of social and ideological pressures created by World War II. [From "Who Did It?" in *The Michigan Chronicle*, July 3, 1943. Selections from *The Michigan Chronical* are reprinted by permission.]

A useless controversy is taking place among our leaders over the issue of who or what was responsible for the racial clash last week that established a new record for American savagery. Any analysis of the forces at work in this community and the most cursory review of the elements of our population will reveal enough dynamite to blow us to bits. To single out any one specific factor and insist that it alone caused the riot is to overlook some very important aspects of our situation and to be guilty of undue over-simplification.

We have long warned that there are active pro-fascists in Detroit whom you may label Klansmen or what you will and that these pro-fascist elements must be routed for the common good. It is naive to believe that this important war arsenal has no fifth-columnists. Hitler knows how important local war industries are to the cause of the United Nations, and, if he doesn't, he is a bigger fool than any of us dare hope at this juncture.

Further we all know that for hundreds of years before Hitler anti-Negro sentiment has been woven into the social fabric of American life. We know that one of the worst manifestations of that anti-Negro sentiment is the unwritten jim crow law which serves to oppress Negroes and to place a wrought iron ceiling over Negro development and progress. While most of the repressive measures against us were created in the Southland, the North has rapidly adopted these measures in order to solve the problems created by the influx of colored families from Dixie.

Another important aspect of this picture is the phenomenal rise of the Negro people themselves. Actually we have made progress faster than the dominant group has been prepared to expect. The comforting illusion of many whites that Negroes were really inferior has been knocked into a cock hat and they see today that if the Negro is really given opportunities he will take adequate and sometimes extraordinary advantage of them. The truth is breaking in upon the mind of white America that the colored Americans are proving the democratic axiom that all men are created equal. Many whites hate to be robbed of their cherished illusions.

Given this state of affairs, we must take note of the tremendous implications of this great war and how they affect the status quo of race relations. The very character of this war—a war for freedom, for democracy, for liberation—has of necessity produced profound changes in our own thinking and has accelerated the hopes of all of us for a new America and even a new world.

Two apparently irresistible forces are meeting in our society and the democratic forces are challenging the forces of reaction. This is what is meant when we refer to the World War as a world revolution. The increased tension between Negroes and some elements in the white population which results in rioting is a manifestation of the deep conflict between democracy and fascism. From this point of view we cannot dismiss the Detroit riot as a queer accident, as some fluke of circumstance and common sense alone dictates that we think this thing through and act with reason rather than with our natural promptings.

During World War I black troops were stationed in a number of Southern army camps. While they objected to the jim crow treatment which they received in nearby towns, local whites felt insulted and threatened by the presence of black soldiers in their midst. This situation had preceded the eruption of black soldiers in Houston in 1917. [Editorial, *Galveston Daily News*, August 25, 1917.]

The negro soldiers who made war on the white people of Houston seem to have had for their casus beli the arrest of a negro woman in their camp. Captain Snow, their commander, says the troops had previously got into an ugly mood because of what they regarded as unfair treatment at the hands of the police officers of Houston. Possibly they had been subjected to petty harassments; the idea that they had been is easily conceivable. But a negro in uniform with an exaggerative sense of the privileges and immunities that uniform confers lacks a vast deal of being an angelic creature, and it is just as easy to conceive that these soldiers gave ample provocation for everything that the police officers had done. But even if it be assumed that the officers, and not the negro soldiers, were responsible for the ill feeling that had been engendered, that assumption can not be made to excuse, nor even condone, the murderous rampage of those soldiers. The larger fact probably is that, regardless of whether their grievance against the police officers at Houston was real or fancied, they made it merely a pretext to give vent to a feeling of racial animosity. Certainly they did not restrict their vengeance to the police officers. They fired promiscuously and counted women and children among their victims.

Secretary Baker has ordered these troops away from Houston. That may be accepted as an acknowledgement that he ought never to have sent them there. Racial antipathy is intensified and made active when a soldier's uniform is put upon a negro. This is not true alone of the South. There have been clashes and disturbances in the North that prove that even the people of that section are not impervious to the arrogance and pugnacity with which the uniform seems often to inspire the negro. The Southern people are merely quicker in their resentment. And it is this fact which makes it always a blunder to station negro soldiers in Southern communities. There are enough instances in the history of the last ten or twenty years to make a full-sized warning against the imprudence of stationing negro troops in Southern communities, but the war department authorities were evidently heedless of it.

[From "The Cause Of and Remedy For Race Riots," by the Editors, *The Messenger*, September, 1919.]

Lastly, military causes have not been without their effect in the production of race riots. For four and one-half years the religion of violence had been taught to both white and black people of America. War has engendered the spirit of violence. The transition from shooting a white German is not very far from shooting a white American. Besides, Negroes hate American whites, but they almost uniformly report that the Germans were among the fairest and the best people they have ever met. They like the Germans as well as the French. Everybody overseas was better to the Negro soldier than the white American. Hence the Negro returned with vengeance and hatred for the white American in his breast. He noted the difference in the treatment abroad from that he got at home. The white American also noted this difference. The Negro favored it: the white American disapproved of the French fraternal spirit. Hence, the clash. Upon returning home, the Negro found conditions worse than when he left, despite his fight to "make the world safe for democracy." He is dissatisfied with his reward for his participation in the war. Not knowing President Wilson, he took him at his word. He wants to make the world safe for democracy, and is therefore determined to make America safe for himself. He secured the knowledge of the art and value of organization. And he is determined to use this knowledge and art in the interest of himself.

Dr. J. N. Sharp, acting assistant surgeon U.S. volunteers connected with the Freedman's Bureau, testified before a Senate committee investigating the Memphis riot in 1866. Dr. Sharp spoke of attitudes he perceived to be prevalent in Memphis after the Civil War. [From Select Committee Report, *Memphis Riots and Massacres.* Report No. 101, 39th Cong., 1st Sess., p. 158.]

2111. You have spoken of the manner in which the negroes have been arrested by the police. Do you know whether any efforts have been made upon the part of citizens here to prevent that brutality? I have never heard of any.

2112. Is there any public sentiment that would warrant citizens so disposed from interfering to prevent such brutality? I do not think there is.

2113. Do you think it would be safe for any one who witnessed an outrage of that sort to be active in bringing police officers to punishment? No, sir; I would not want my name known if there was not military protection here.

2114. You have spoken of the manner in which the mob of firemen, policemen, and citizens acted—could that mob have acted as they did without a public sentiment to back them? No, sir; if the mayor of the city had said quit, they would have quit at any time.

2115. Where is the public sentiment? In what sort of people? It is confined to the southern people; not only to such people as the mob was composed of, but to such as the Argus and Avalanche people.

2116. Do you know whether any of the papers here that represented the great mass of people here have ever denounced this conduct of the police in arresting negroes in a brutal manner? No, sir. Some of our papers did, in effect, advocate it. Along last fall for two months they made the citizens believe that the negroes were all going to rise before Christmas, and advising citizens, if they did, to clean them out. They were constantly stirring up the people in this way. I was among the negroes of the 3d heavy artillery at that time, and I never heard a breath of such a thing from them.

2117. Has there been any behavior on the part of the negro soldiers or resident negroes to warrant any suspicion that they intended mischief? No, sir, not to my knowledge.

By the CHAIRMAN:

2118. What was the object of these continued predictions of insurrection about Christmas? I do not know, unless it was to get up just such a mob as was raised about the first of this month. I was talking with a man in reference to this very matter. He swore that the citizens of Memphis ought to "clean out every God damned negro in the city." I said to him that will not do. The negroes must have protection as well as the whites. He replied they might as well do it now as at any other time; "we will have to do it eventually." I told him we had no right to do anything of that sort; that we had law, and I thought all law-abiding citizens ought to discountenance all such proceedings. This was on the evening of the first day of the riot. He said that as soon as the soldiers were away they would have to do it, and he thought the people of Memphis might as well rise up and clean them out now as at any time.

"The Spirit of Lawlessness"

Boom-town conditions could provide an excellent explosive mixture. [From "The End of Argonaut Days," editorial in *The Tulsa Tribune*, June 5, 1921.]

Tulsa is the capital of an El Dorado. It boasts of its wealth. But Tulsa is better than a city of millionaires: it is a city of generally distributed wealth and has the highest per capita wealth of any city in the world. Tulsa is young. When this territory came into statehood fourteen years ago Tulsa was a village. Today it is an ambitious little metropolis of one hundred thousand people. While this is a rich agricultural country it is the mineral wealth that has given this city its remarkable growth and put it at least fifty years ahead. Men have come to Tulsa to make money. Today they see a new duty—to make a good city. Tulsa today is just emerging from her Argonaut era. Heretofore the average Tulsan has been too busy with his own private affairs to invest his conscience in his citizenship. The result has been that law enforcement has been lax for years. Gambling and bootlegging and hi-jacking have gone on little molested. And some of the time protected by the police. This has developed a lawless element.

Lack of law enforcement has permitted a bad negro element to develop a disrespect both for county and city officials and a lack of fear of all officers of the law.

Only recently a group of public-spirited citizens protested against these traditional conditions and the office of the attorney general of the state has been making searching investigations into the lack of efficiency of the city and county officers.

The city administration investigated itself and found itself practically spotless.

"Niggertown" has been a cesspool of iniquity. There most of the criminal of the community, both white and black, found harbor. There crimes were plotted. There an uprising has long been in process of planning. There this disorder began. The bad elements among the negroes, long plotting and planning and collecting guns and ammunition, brought this upon Tulsa just as the winds gather into a cyclone and sweep upon a city. This bad element among the negroes must learn that this is not a city of, for and by their kind. NEVER.

Could any city have been as decadent as a Congressional investigating committee contended East St. Louis had been on the eve of its riot in 1917? [From *East St. Louis Riots, Congressional Record,* Vol. 56, pt. 9, pp. 8828–29.]

In the history of corrupt politics in this country there never has been a more shameless debauchery of the electorate nor a more vicious alliance between the agencies and beneficiaries of crime than for years existed in East St. Louis. It is a disgraceful chapter. It puts an ineffaceable brand on every man engaged in the conspiracy. Its contamination, spreading from a reservoir of corruption in the city hall, filtered through carefully laid conduits into every street and alley; into the hotels where girls, mere children of 15 years of age, were violated; into the low dance halls where schoolgirls listened to lewd songs and engaged in lascivious dances, and in the interval retired to assignation rooms with the drunken brutes who frequented these resorts; into the gambling houses where poorly paid workmen were robbed of their daily earnings; into the 350 saloons which kept open on Sunday, many of them running without license; into the barrel houses, where the vilest of whisky was sold in bottles, the resort of vagrants and drunkards, rendezvous of criminals and schools of crime.

This corruption palsied the hands of prominent officials whose duty it was to enforce the law. Lawyers became protectors of criminals; the courts were shields for the highwaymen, the prostitute, the gambler, the sneak thief and the murderer. The higher courts were not free from this baneful influence, which invaded all ranks and brought them to its low level.

Local judges were found who would take straw bonds that the worst criminals might escape; exacting only costs, two-thirds going into the pockets of the judge and one-third into the waiting palm of the chief of police.

A police force is never better than the police commissioner; and the police commissioners, in turn reflect the character and wishes of the mayor. If a city has a mayor of courage and ability, who is not the weak and willing prey of political crooks and grafters, he is certain to appoint a board of police commissioners who will name policemen intelligent enough to know the law and brave and honest enough to enforce it.

East St. Louis was doubly unfortunate. In the person of Mayor Mollman it had an executive who obeyed orders from a gang of conscienceless politicians of both political parties, who were exploiting the city for their own aggrandizement, careless alike of its good name, its security or its prosperity. They were harpies who closed their eyes to the corruption that saturated every department of the public service and fattened on its festering carcass. Without conscience and without shame they led the mayor into devious paths, tempted him with assurances of political support for his future ambitions, packed the police force with men whose incompetency was only surpassed by their venality, and so circumscribed him with flattery and encouraged his cupidity that they were able to take the reins of government from his feeble hands and guide it to suit their own foul and selfish purposes.

The great majority of the police force appointed by Mayor Mollman's board of police commissioners had served an apprenticeship as connivers at corrupt elections; as protectors of lawless saloons, and hotels run openly as assignation houses. They turned criminals loose at the dictation of politicians, and divided with grafting justices of the peace the fines that should have gone into the treasury.

This was the general charter of the police force of the city of East
St. Louis on July 1, 1917, when the spirit of lawlessness, long smoldering, burst into flame.

The Police: Friction in Social Control

Differential police treatment generates as much friction as any single
feature of life in a black ghetto. [From Rossi, et al., "Between Black
and White—The Faces of American Institutions in the Ghetto," *Supplemental Studies for The National Advisory Commission on Civil
Disorders* (Washington, D.C.: Government Printing Office, 1968), pp.
107–8.]

. . . It is clear that police quite frequently intervene in domestic
quarrels and break up loitering groups. This often places them in
delicate situations where they interfere with groups of people who may
consider their own behavior normal and legitimate, and at the least
not a proper subject of forceful interference. The tension that may be
created by indelicate actions in these circumstances is hardly helped
by the frequent practice of placing the least skilled policemen in the
higher crime areas.

The other activities that policemen report frequently engaging in
seldom can be expected to endear them to the residents. About a third
are frequently stopping people to question or frisk them, implying
thereby that the person stopped is suspected of some crime or potential crime. Almost a fourth report frequently searching without a
warrant, further indicating to a great number of residents that they
do not merit the justification of due cause to a court. More than a
third frequently interrogate suspected drug users. Since the use of the
less habituating drugs is considered less onerous by ghetto norms than
by white middle class standards, such interrogation is easily inter-
preted as the imposition of alien and unjustified standards of conduct
upon a powerless people. The police, then, are constantly interfering
with many of the day-to-day activities of a significant portion of the
residents of the neighborhood. It is quite understandable how this
imposition—whether justified or not—could generate a considerable
level of hostility.

Some degree of hostility can be expected to be generated by the
regular surveillance activity of the police. Those who were innocent
of any intended or actual wrong-doing are likely to dislike being
stopped and frisked. Indeed, the probability of a person who is stopped

and frisked by the police being innocent is much larger than the probability of being caught in some illegal activity. The President's Commission on Law Enforcement and the Administration of Justice reported that in some high crime areas only ten per cent of those stopped and frisked were found to be carrying a gun, and another ten per cent were found to be carrying knives. The policemen in our sample claim a higher success rate, as the evidence in Table 6.8 indicates. The median number of persons found to be "carrying something that might lead to a crime" when stopped and frisked is 5.1, according to our policemen. Furthermore, the police also claim that a median of 3.5 individuals were found to be wanted criminals or to have committed some illegal act.

We think it would be safe to assume that the policemen are claiming more positive results from the stop and frisk procedure than is actually the case. In any event, the majority of persons stopped are innocent of any wrong doing. If the rate of stopping and frisking in the Negro community is very high, then it would not take long for the police to antagonize a large number of residents. Interestingly, there were no differences between Negro and white policemen in the reported median frequency with which suspicions were verified in frisks.

*   *   *

The typical interaction between policemen and suspect, when people are questioned and frisked, is not congenial. Only nine per cent of the policemen report that people they stop are usually fully cooperative. . . . More than eighty per cent admit that the usual reaction is at least a dislike of being frisked. Forty-one per cent of the policemen report that they usually have to use threats or force to get the suspect to respond adequately. Eleven per cent find that their suspects usually physically resist their efforts to question and frisk. Such responses from suspects would be expected from hardened criminals. But in a situation on which a majority of those stopped are neither carrying weapons nor are criminals, and in which thirty-four per cent of the policemen frequently stop and frisk people, it is clear that considerable hostility is generated among many others than those directly engaged in criminal behavior.

The editor of a black newspaper expressed such indignation and hostility. [Editorial, *Tulsa Star,* January 1, 1920.]

The reprehensible action of certain white policemen who persist in invading the colored section of the city, over-riding Colored policemen who have been assigned to duty in this district has just about reached the overflow point, and unless something is done by superior officers to check this practice serious trouble will certainly result.

Numerous occasions might be mentioned where hot-headed soft-skulled white officers have unceremoniously entered business places in the Colored section and without any kind of legal excuse or explanation search the person of the patrons of such places, very often when Colored officers are in or near the place, and without invitation or permission from the proprietors.

Sooner or later this practice will provoke a killing of these legal hijacks and when that happens it will require eternal vigilences to prevent a serious race conflict—something that no good [sic] desires to see.

There have been several complaints among Colored people lately about white officers who have exceeded their authority in their conduct in the Colored section. It seems to be a well established policy with these officers to go out of their way to misuse Colored people. One night this week the editor of this paper was held up by five white officers while he was in a taxi within half a block of the police station and his life threatened because he had the manhood to protest against their high handed methods. It was an easy matter for these brave officers with drawn guns to intercept a law-abiding citizen almost within the door of the police station, but their vigilence counts for naught against the thieves and things [sic] who are making life miserable for the citizens of Tulsa. It is high time that this city be made safe for law-abiding people who demand protection not only from thieves and things [sic] who use the cover of night and the masks to ply their trade without regard for law, but from another class of the same animals who are cloaked with the authority of law.

It must be said to the credit of Inspector Daley and Chief Gustafson however, that such action on the part of these officers has been, not only without their knowledge but strictly against their specific orders, and now that their attention has been called to it, we may expect a marked improvement in the conduct of those against whom complaints have been made. These officers will be given to understand that in the discharge of their duties they must not lose sight of the fact that all citizens have legal rights that even police officers must respect.

Man, Age About 33

[From Kenneth B. Clark, *Dark Ghetto* (New York: Harper & Row, Publishers, 1965; London: Victor Gollancz Ltd.), pp. 4–5. Copyright © 1965 by Kenneth B. Clark. Selections from *Dark Ghetto* are reprinted by permission of the publishers.]

The white cops, they have a damn sadistic nature. They are really a sadistic type of people and we, I mean me, myself, we don't need them here in Harlem. We don't need them! They don't do the neighborhood any good. They deteriorate the neighborhood. They start more violence than any other people start. They start violence, that's right. A bunch of us could be playing some music, or dancing, which we have as an outlet for ourselves. We can't dance in the house, we don't have clubs or things like that. So we're out on the sidewalk, right on the sidewalk; we might feel like dancing, or one might want to play something on his horn. Right away here comes a cop. "You're disturbing the peace!" No one has said anything, you understand; no one has made a complaint. Everyone is enjoying themselves. But here comes one cop, and he'll want to chase everyone. And gets mad. I mean, he gets mad! We aren't mad. He comes into the neighborhood, aggravated and mad.

Man, Age About 35

Last night, for instance, the officer stopped some fellows on 125th Street, Car No. ——, that was the number of the car, and because this fellow spoke so nicely for his protection and his rights, the officer said, "All right, everybody get off the street or inside!" Now, it's very hot. We don't have air-conditioned apartments in most of these houses up here, so where are we going if we get off the streets? We can't go back in the house because we almost suffocate. So we sit down on the curb, or stand on the sidewalk, or on the steps, things like that, till the wee hours of the morning, especially in the summer when it's too hot to go up. Now where were we going? But he came out with his nightstick and wants to beat people on the head, and wanted to—he arrested one fellow. The other fellow said, "Well, I'll move, but you don't have to talk to me like a dog." I think we should all get together —everybody—all get together and every time one draws back his stick to do something to us, or hits one of us on the head, take the stick and hit *him* on *his* head, so he'll know how it feels to be hit on the head, or kill him, if necessary. Yes, kill him, if necessary. That's how I feel. There is no other way to deal with this man. The only way you can deal with him is the way he has been dealing with us.

[Editorial, *Galveston Daily News*, August 26, 1917.]

The reason for such an investigation lies in the fact that a good deal of our race trouble in the South is caused by unnecessary harshness on the part of police officers in their dealings with negroes. In too many instances they act as if they were the agents of vengeance rather than of justice. They can be firm and sufficiently vigorous in performing their difficult and sometimes dangerous duty without being brutal. The proof of this is that they customarily act with this restraint in their dealings with white people. But they exhibit many exceptions to this rule when it comes to dealing with negroes. Police officers who can not assert their authority without brutality in the case of negroes ought to be eliminated from every police force in the South because they make the clubs given them as weapons into incendiary torches. Without intending it, and perhaps often without knowing it, they more often disturb than preserve the public peace.

Black Ghetto Pathology

The following selections describe some of the pathological conditions of black ghettos. [From the Kerner Report, pp. 124–26, 133–35.]

Unemployment rates among Negroes have declined from a post-Korean War high of 12.6 per cent in 1958 to 8.2 per cent in 1967. Among married Negro men, the unemployment rate for 1967 was down to 3.2 per cent.

Notwithstanding this decline, unemployment rates for Negroes are still double those for whites in every category, including married men, as they have been throughout the post-war period. Moreover, since 1954, even during the current unprecedented period of sustained economic growth, unemployment among Negroes has been continuously above the 6 per cent "recession" level widely regarded as a sign of serious economic weakness when prevalent for the entire work force.

* * *

Even more important perhaps than unemployment is the related problem of the undesirable nature of many jobs open to Negroes. Negro workers are concentrated in the lower-skilled and lowest-paying occupations. These jobs often involve substandard wages, great instability and uncertainty of tenure, extremely low status in the eyes of both employer and employee, little or no chance for meaningful advancement, and unpleasant or exhausting duties.

* * *

In disadvantaged areas, employment conditions for Negroes are in a chronic state of crisis. Surveys in low-income neighborhoods of nine

large cities made by the Department of Labor late in 1966 revealed
that the rate of unemployment there was 9.3 per cent, compared to
7.3 per cent for Negroes generally and 3.3 per cent for whites. Moreover, a high proportion of the persons living in these areas were
"underemployed," that is they were either part-time workers looking
for full-time employment, or full-time workers earning less than $3000
per year, or had dropped out of the labor force. The Department of
Labor estimated that this underemployment is 2½ times greater than
the number unemployed in these areas. Therefore, the "subemploy-
ment rate," including both the unemployed and the underemployed,
was about 32.7 per cent in the nine areas surveyed, or 8.8 times greater
than the overall unemployment rate for all U.S. workers.

*   *   *

Nothing is more fundamental to the quality of life in any area than
the sense of personal security of its residents, and nothing affects this
more than crime.

In general, crime rates in large cities are much higher than in other
areas of the country. Within such cities, crime rates are higher in
disadvantaged Negro areas than anywhere else.

*   *   *

Two facts are crucial to an understanding of the effects of high
crime rates in racial ghettos; most of these crimes are committed by
a small minority of the residents, and the principal victims are the
residents themselves. Throughout the United States, the great majority
of crimes committed by Negroes involve other Negroes as victims. A
special tabulation made by the Chicago Police Department for the
President's Crime Commission indicated that over 85 per cent of the
crimes committed against persons by Negroes between September,
1965, and March, 1966, involved Negro victims.

As a result, the majority of law-abiding citizens who live in disadvantaged Negro areas face much higher probabilities of being
victimized than residents of most higher income areas, including almost
all suburbs. For nonwhites, the probability of suffering from any index
crime except larceny is 78 per cent higher than for whites. The probability of being raped is 3.7 times higher among nonwhite women,
and the probability of being robbed is 3.5 times higher for nonwhites
in general.

[From Clark, *Dark Ghetto*, p. 12.]

The pathologies of the ghetto community perpetuate themselves
through cumulative ugliness, deterioration, and isolation and strengthen

the Negro's sense of worthlessness, giving testimony to his impotence. Yet the ghetto is not totally isolated. The mass media—radio, television, moving pictures, magazines, and the press—penetrate, indeed, invade the ghetto in continuous and inevitable communication, largely one-way, and project the values and aspirations, the manners and the style of the larger white-dominated society. Those who are required to live in congested and rat-infested homes are aware that others are not so dehumanized. Young people in the ghetto are aware that other young people have been taught to read, that they have been prepared for college, and can compete successfully for white-collar, managerial, and executive jobs. Whatever accommodations they themselves must make to the negative realities which dominate their own lives, they know consciously or unconsciously that their fate is not the common fate of mankind. They tend to regard their predicament as a consequence of personal disability or as an inherent and imposed powerlessness which all Negroes share.

The privileged white community is at great pains to blind itself to conditions of the ghetto, but the residents of the ghetto are not themselves blind to life as it is outside of the ghetto. They observe that others enjoy a better life, and this knowledge brings a conglomerate of hostility, despair, and hope. If the ghetto could be contained totally, the chances of social revolt would be decreased, if not eliminated, but it cannot be contained and the outside world intrudes. The Negro lives in part in the world of television and motion pictures, bombarded by the myths of the American middle class, often believing as literal truth their pictures of luxury and happiness, and yet at the same time confronted by a harsh world of reality where the dreams do not come true or change into nightmares. The discrepancy between the reality and the dream burns into their consciousness. The oppressed can never be sure whether their failures reflect personal inferiority or the fact of color. This persistent and agonizing conflict dominates their lives.

[From *The Negro in Chicago*, p. 115.]

There are residence districts of Chicago adjacent to those occupied by Negroes in which hostility to Negroes is so marked that the latter not only find it impossible to live there, but expose themselves to danger even by passing through. There are no hostile organizations in these neighborhoods, and active antagonism is usually confined to gang lawlessness. Such a neighborhood is that west of Wentworth Avenue, extending roughly from Twenty-second to Sixty-third streets. The number of Negroes living there is small, and most of them live on Ada, Aberdeen, and Loomis streets, south of Fifty-seventh Street. In the section immediately west of Wentworth Avenue and thus adjoining the densest Negro residence area in the city, practically no Negroes live. In addition to intense hostility, there is a lack of desirable houses. Wentworth Avenue has long been regarded as a strict boundary line separating white and Negro residence areas. The district has many "athletic clubs." The contact of Negroes and whites comes when Negroes must pass to and from their work at the Stock Yards and at other industries located in the district. It was in this district that the largest number of riot clashes occurred. Several Negroes have been murdered here, and numbers have been beaten by gangs of young men and boys. A white man was killed by one of two Negroes returning from work in that district, who declared that they had been intimidated by the slain man. Speaking of this district, the principal of the Raymond School, a branch of which is located west of Wentworth Avenue, said that antagonism of the district against Negroes appeared to have been handed down through tradition. He said:

We get a good deal of the gang spirit in the new school on the other side of Wentworth Avenue. There seems to be an inherited antagonism. Wentworth Avenue is the gang line. They seem to feel that to trespass on either side of that line is ground for trouble. While colored pupils who come to the school for manual training are not troubled in the school, they have to be escorted over the line, not because of trouble from members of the school, but groups of boys outside the school. To give another illustration, we took a little kindergarten group over to the park. One little six-year-old girl was struck in the face by a man. A policeman chased but failed to catch him. The condition is a tradition. It is handed down.

[From the Kerner Report, pp. 129–30.]

With the father absent and the mother working, many ghetto children spend the bulk of their time on the streets—the streets of a crime-ridden, violence-prone, and poverty-stricken world. The image of success in this world is not that of the "solid citizen," the responsible husband and father, but rather that of the "hustler" who promotes his own interests by exploiting others. The dope sellers and the numbers runners are the "successful" men because their earnings far outstrip those men who try to climb the economic ladder in honest ways.

Young people in the ghetto are acutely conscious of a system which appears to offer rewards to those who illegally exploit others, and failure to those who struggle under traditional responsibilities. Under these circumstances, many adopt exploitation and the "hustle" as a way of life, disclaiming both work and marriage in favor of casual and temporary liaisons. This pattern reinforces itself from one generation to the next, creating a "culture of poverty" and an ingrained cynicism about society and its institutions.

"A Toast to Harlem"

Langston Hughes created the Harlem Everyman, Simple, through whom he told some of the most revealing stories about life in Harlem. Let Simple speak for himself. [From Langston Hughes, "A Toast to Harlem," in *The Best of Simple* (New York: Hill and Wang, Inc., 1961). Copyright © 1961 by Langston Hughes. Reprinted by permission of Hill and Wang, Inc. and Harold Ober Associates, Inc.]

QUIET can seem unduly loud at times. Since nobody at the bar was saying a word during a lull in the bright blues-blare of the Wishing Well's usually overworked juke box, I addressed my friend Simple.

"Since you told me last night you are an Indian, explain to me how it is you find yourself living in a furnished room in Harlem, my brave buck, instead of on a reservation?"

"I am a colored Indian," said Simple.

"In other words, a Negro."

"A Black Foot Indian, daddy-o, not a red one. Anyhow, Harlem is the place I always did want to be. And if it wasn't for the landladies, I would be happy. That's a fact! I love Harlem."

"What is it you love about Harlem?"

"It's so full of Negroes," said Simple. "I feel like I got protection."

"From what?"

"From white folks," said Simple. "Furthermore, I like Harlem because it belongs to me."

"Harlem does not belong to you. You don't own the houses in Harlem. They belong to white folks."

"I might not own 'em," said Simple, "but I live in 'em. It would take an atom bomb to get me out."

"Or a depression," I said.

"I would not move for no depression. No, I would not go back down South, not even to Baltimore. I am in Harlem to stay! You say the houses ain't mine. Well, the sidewalk is—and don't nobody push me off. The cops don't even say, 'Move on,' hardly no more. They learned something from them Harlem riots. They used to beat your head right in public, but now they only beat it after they get you down to the stationhouse. And they don't beat it then if they think you know a colored congressman."

"Harlem has a few Negro leaders," I said.

"Elected by my *own* vote," said Simple. "Here I ain't scared to vote —that's another thing I like about Harlem. I also like it because we've got subways and it does not take all day to get downtown, neither are you Jim Crowed on the way. Why, Negroes is running some of these subway trains. This morning I rode the A Train down to 34th Street. There were a Negro driving it, making ninety miles a hour. That cat *were really driving* that train! Every time he flew by one of them local stations looks like he was saying, 'Look at me! This train is mine!' That cat were gone, ole man. Which is another reason why I like Harlem! Sometimes I run into Duke Ellington on 125th Street and I say, 'What you know there, Duke?' Duke says, 'Solid, ole man.' He does not know me from Adam, but he speaks. One day I saw Lena Horne coming out of the Hotel Theresa and I said, 'Hubba! Hubba!' Lena smiled. Folks is friendly in Harlem. I feel like I got the world in a jug and the stopper in my hand! So drink a toast to Harlem!"

Simple lifted his glass of beer:

> Here's to Harlem!
> They say Heaven is Paradise.
> If Harlem ain't Heaven,
> Then a mouse ain't mice!

"Heaven is a state of mind," I commented.

"It sure is *mine*," said Simple, draining his glass. "From Central Park to 179th, from river to river, Harlem is mine! Lots of white folks is scared to come up here, too, after dark."

"That is nothing to be proud of," I said.

"I am sorry white folks is scared to come to Harlem, but I am scared to go around some of *them*. Why, for instant, in my home town once before I came North to live, I was walking down the street when a white woman jumped out of her door and said, 'Boy, get away from here because I am scared of you.'

"I said, 'Why?'

"She said, 'Because you are black.'

"I said, 'Lady, I am scared of you because you are white.' I went on down the street, but I kept wishing I was blacker—so I could of scared that lady to death. So help me, I did. Imagine somebody talking about they is scared of me because I am black! I got more reason to be scared of white folks than they have of me."

"Right," I said.

"The white race drug me over here from Africa, slaved me, freed me, lynched me, starved me during the depression, Jim Crowed me during the war—then they come talking about they is scared of me! Which is why I am glad I have got one spot to call my own where I hold sway—Harlem. Harlem, where I can thumb my nose at the world!"

"You talk just like a Negro nationalist," I said.

"What's that?"

"Someone who wants Negroes to be on top."

"When everybody else keeps me on the *bottom,* I don't see why I shouldn't want to be on top. I will, too, someday."

"That's the spirit that causes wars," I said.

"I would not mind a war if I could win it. White folks fight, lynch, and enjoy themselves."

"There you go," I said. "That old *race-against-race* jargon. There'll never be peace that way. The world tomorrow ought to be a world where everybody gets along together. The least we can do is extend a friendly hand."

"Every time I extend my hand I get put back in my place. You know them poetries about the black cat that tried to be friendly with the white one:

> The black cat said to the white cat,
> "Let's sport around the town."
> The white cat said to the black cat,
> "You better set your black self down!"

"Unfriendliness of that nature should not exist," I said. "Folks ought to live like neighbors."

"You're talking about what ought to be. But as long as what *is* is —and Georgia is Georgia—I will take Harlem for mine. At least, if trouble comes, I will have *my own window* to shoot from."

"I refuse to argue with you any more," I said. "What Harlem ought to hold out to the world from its windows is a friendly hand, not a belligerent attitude."

"It will not be my attitude I will have out my window," said Simple.

☞ **5** ☜

THE MATCH

Given the tradition of racial violence and the existence of a powder keg, the potential for explosions in American society is great. Some specific incident, which in and of itself may or may not be worthy of marked attention, supplies the spark. Sometimes the incidents themselves are serious—an actual or threatened lynching, a clash between troops and police, a drowning, an altercation over an arrest that results in gunplay—but they become riots because of a chain reaction that spreads rapidly to the larger community. Often the incidents do not start seriously, but quickly flare into overtly hostile acts—an arrest, a vice raid, a fist fight can escalate into mob activity.

Word of an incident spreads. It gets distorted in the telling. In an atmosphere of tension rumors are accepted at face value. It is at this point that a few agitators may spring into action; but be they whites or blacks, they cannot exceed the limits of their gathering audience's credulity. Unfortunately for domestic tranquility, these limits are high: black men are all rapists and white cops are all sadistic brutes. The reaction of growing mobs, be they white or black, quickly goes beyond outrage over the particular incident. The accumulated insecurities and grievances, fancied or real, of the powder keg have been ignited. From a variety of narrators, here are several versions of incidents that have supplied the match.

Merely the Pretext

The Federal Conscription Act in 1863 provoked considerable furor, especially since it allowed eligible draftees to avoid service by paying $300. Mobs of working-class men, especially Irish-Americans, disrupted the first public drawings in New York City in July, and plunged the city into the bloodiest riot of American history. Armed conflicts raged for over a week, and while it was impossible to fix the exact death toll, all estimates ran upwards of 1,000 killed. [From an editorial, "The Riots," in *Harper's Weekly*, August 1, 1863, p. 482.]

It is about as idle now to argue the question of the $300 clause in the Conscription Act as it is to debate the abstract right of secession. Before Monday night the riot had got far beyond the question of the draft. Within an hour after the destruction of the Provost-Marshal's office the rioters had forgotten all about the $300 question, and were engrossed with villainous projects of murder, arson, and pillage. It was not in order to avoid the draft that the colored orphan asylum was burnt; that private houses were sacked; that inoffensive colored persons were beaten, mutilated, and murdered; that Brooks's clothing establishment and a score of other smaller stores were pillaged; that private citizens were robbed in open daylight in the public streets, beaten and maimed; that the metropolis of the country was kept for nearly a week in a state of agonizing terror and suspense. For these outrages the draft was merely the pretext; the cause was the natural turbulence of a heterogeneous populace, aggravated by the base teachings of despicable politicians and their newspaper organs.

Lynching and Riots

In 1906, during the height of one of the bitterest racist battles in Georgia's political history, Atlantans were treated to an amazing assortment of daily atrocity stories. During the six weeks immediately preceeding the riot in that city, the *Atlanta Constitution* carried on its front page 106 accounts of brutal personal assaults. Of these, only 14 occurred in greater Atlanta, over half were tales of whites murdering and raping whites or committing suicide elsewhere, and 10 per cent involved black violence against whites. Note that this was only on page one (the inside pages presented a longer catalogue of horrors), and that the *Constitution* was Atlanta's most conservative newspaper. The following selections set the tone of the prevailing atmosphere of hysteria and describe the incidents which touched off the Atlanta riot of September, 1906. [From Ray Stannard Baker, *Following the Color Line* (New York: Doubleday, Page & Company, 1908), pp. 8–9.]

The next view I got was through the eyes of one of the able Negroes of the South, Bishop Gaines of the African Methodist Episcopal

Church. He is now an old man, but of imposing presence. Of wide attainments, he has travelled in Europe, he owns much property, and rents houses to white tenants. He told me of services he had held some time before in south Georgia. Approaching the church one day through the trees, he suddenly encountered a white woman carrying water from a spring. She dropped her pail instantly, screamed, and ran up the path toward her house.

"If I had been some Negroes," said Bishop Gaines, "I should have turned and fled in terror; the alarm would have been given, and it is not unlikely that I should have had a posse of white men with blood-hounds on my trail. If I had been caught what would my life have been worth? The woman would have identified me—and what could I have said? But I did not run. I stepped out in the path, held up one hand and said:

"'Don't worry, madam, I am Bishop Gaines, and I am holding services here in this church.' So she stopped running and I apologised for having startled her."

[Front page, *Atlanta Constitution*, August 25, 1906.]

ANOTHER GIRL ASSAULTED;
LOCAL MILITIA COMPANY
GUARDING DECATUR JAIL

Eighteen-Year-Old School Teacher in Adamsville District
Attacked by Negro Yesterday

SCREAMS OF MISS WAITES
SCARED HER ASSAILANT
AND SAVED HER HONOR

Posse Was Quickly Organized and Pursuit Given,
but Up to a Late Hour No Arrest Had Been Made
—Attack Near Scene of Recent Murder

A negro attempted to attack Miss Mittie Waites, a school teacher at Adamsville, 9 miles from the city, yesterday afternoon about 2 o'clock and only the screams of the young lady saved her from a probable assault.

Miss Waites was alone in the woods at the time, several hundred yards from her home, when the negro tried to attack her. She screamed and ran when the negro advanced upon her and he turned into the woods near by and disappeared.

The affair was quickly told in the neighborhood and a posse of citizens was organized. A telephone message to the city notified the county police and Chief Turner soon had his men on the scene.

The woods near by were scoured, but from last accounts the negro had not been captured.

Miss Waites was greatly excited and came near having nervous prostration from her experience.

Yesterday afternoon she left the house of her mother and went to a spring in the woods to get a bucket of water. She was stooping over the spring, filling the bucket, when she heard a noise, and upon looking up she saw a large, heavily built, black negro looking at her. As she arose to her feet the negro started toward her. She dropped the bucket and started to run. She screamed and the negro called to her to stop.

This only frightened her the more and she continued to run and to call for help.

After following the young lady a few yards the negro became alarmed at her continued screaming and he left the path and disappeared in a thicket.

Miss Waites is the 18-year-old daughter of Mr. Waites, who is now farming in Adamsville district and who was formerly a deputy sheriff at the court house.

Where the negro tried to attack Miss Waites yesterday afternoon is not far from the spot where Amos Moody was murdered last Saturday afternoon. The people in the district are still worked up over the crime, and when they heard of the attempt to attack Miss Waites they were incensed. If the negro can be caught and identified he would not have much chance of even reaching a prison alive.

[Editorial, *Atlanta News*, August 26, 1906.]

MEN OF GEORGIA, BESTIR YOURSELVES!

There is no crime under heaven so base, so brutal, so infamous, so hellish in its purpose and so horrible in its design and effect as the crime of assault on an innocent, defenseless white girl or woman.

Such a crime is a violation of the sanctity of womanhood.

Women are the mothers of nations and the hope of civilization. They are the bulwark of life and religion.

They are the angels of the earth and the best of the human family. A true, good woman is beyond compare.

Her honor and her virtue and her innocence are the greatest prize and blessing bestowed upon man.

When the world is dark and dreary, and life seems hopeless, woman in the form of mother, wife, daughter, sweetheart, or friend and companion, saves man from despair.

Much of the effort of man's life is made for women.

Man would be a wild beast of the woods except for womankind.

Her gentleness, her charity, her help, her religion, her love and loyalty, make life worth while.

To contemplate a brutal, black fiend and devil violating the sacred person of such a woman as we have described is almost beyond the mind.

It does not seem possible that such a crime against nature and against noble womanhood could be tolerated by the power which rules mankind and all civilization.

To think of the awful crimes being committed against our women is alarming. It seems that men are justified in adopting the most radical punishment for the perpetrators of such deeds that can be devised this side of the region of fire and brimstone.

It is the duty of all men who appreciate a noble, innocent, true woman, of all men who love their homes, their mothers, their wives, their daughters, and their sweethearts, their friends and companions, to bend every effort and every energy, and every means of running down and capturing, and punishing to the fullest extent, the perpetrators of such deeds as are being shamefully and outrageously committed in the midst of this great people and this civilized community.

Then, to arms! Men of Georgia!

Arouse yourselves and begin anew the search for this imp from hell fire who had invaded one of the white families of this section and cruelly beaten a young woman almost to death in his heinous purpose of assaulting and outraging her, and destroying her honor and her hope, and her right to life, liberty, happiness and innocence.

Up, men, and about!

Search the highways and the hedges, and the woods, swamps, hillsides and everywhere for this fiend in human form, who still runs at large to continue his career of crime and destruction to womanhood.

This black devil should be captured and punished without delay.

There is every inducement for his arrest and conviction.

It is a discredit and a shame upon the community that such brutes as this are allowed to run at large and endanger the lives of our women and girls, who are the greatest joy of life and the greatest hope of our nation.

To arms! Men of Atlanta and Fulton county!

Bestir yourselves and continue the relentless search for this black imp, and stop not until you have located him and sent him to the death which he deserves.

[Baker, *Following the Color Line*, pp. 9–10.]

On the afternoon of the riot the newspapers in flaming headlines chronicled four assaults by Negroes on white women. I had a personal investigation made of each of those cases. Two of them may have been attempts at assaults, but two palpably were nothing more than fright on the part of both the white woman and the Negro. As an instance, in one case an elderly woman, Mrs. Martha Holcombe, going to close her blinds in the evening, saw a Negro on the sidewalk. In a terrible fright she screamed. The news was telephoned to the police station, but before the officials could respond, Mrs. Holcombe telephoned them not to come out. And yet this was one of the "assaults" chronicled in letters five inches high in a newspaper extra.

And finally on this hot Saturday half-holiday, when the country people had come in by hundreds, when everyone was out of doors, when the streets were crowded, when the saloons had been filled since early morning with white men and Negroes, both drinking—certain newspapers in Atlanta began to print extras with big headings announcing new assaults on white women by Negroes. The Atlanta *News* published five such extras, and newsboys cried them through the city:

"Third assault."

"Fourth assault."

The whole city, already deeply agitated, was thrown into a veritable state of panic. The news in the extras was taken as truthful; for the city was not in a mood then for cool investigation. Calls began to come in from every direction for police protection. A loafing Negro in a backyard, who in ordinary times would not have been noticed, became an object of real terror. The police force, too small at best, was thus distracted and separated.

In Atlanta the proportion of men who go armed continually is very large; the pawnshops of Decatur and Peters Streets, with windows like arsenals, furnish the low class of Negroes and whites with cheap revolvers and knives. Every possible element was here, then, for a murderous outbreak. The good citizens, white and black, were far away in their homes; the bad men had been drinking in the dives permitted to exist by the respectable people of Atlanta; and here they were gathered, by night, in the heart of the city.

And, finally, a trivial incident fired the tinder. Fear and vengeance generated it: it was marked at first by a sort of rough, half-drunken horseplay, but when once blood was shed, the brute, which is none too well controlled in the best city, came out and gorged itself. Once permit the shackles of law and order to be cast off, and men, white or black, Christian or pagan, revert to primordial savagery. There is no such thing as an orderly mob.

Crime had been committed by Negroes, but this mob made no attempt to find the criminals: it expressed its blind, unreasoning, uncontrolled race hatred by attacking every man, woman, or boy it saw who had a black face.

In Springfield, Illinois, a riot erupted in 1908 as the result of a prevented lynching. [From "The So-called Race Riot at Springfield," By an Eye-Witness," *Charities and Commons* (September 19, 1908), XX, 709–10.]

A few weeks before the riot, the city was aroused by the murder of a Mr. Ballard, a thoroughly reputable citizen, by a Negro named James, who had been discovered by Mr. Ballard's nineteen year old daughter in her room in the night. Ballard grappled with the Negro, and was stabbed to death with a knife. The Negro was discovered later by a searching party, stupefied with drink, and asleep on the ground. The men who found him kicked and beat him, but no attempt was made to lynch him. He was confined in the jail awaiting trial.

On August 13, Mrs. Hallam, the young wife of a street car conductor, alleged that she was attacked while in her home, in bed, dragged into the yard and outraged. She accused George Richardson, a Negro who had been working on a house near her home. The Negro was taken into custody by the sheriff about noon. At two o'clock he was identified by Mrs. Hallam. Before the sheriff was satisfied with the identification he was compelled to take the Negro to the jail because of threats of violence to his prisoner. The mob began to assemble about the jail, and at four o'clock the crowd numbered about three thousand people. At five o'clock, after an alarm of fire was turned in, the two Negroes, James and Richardson, in view of part of the crowd, were placed in an automobile owned and driven by Mr. Loper who had frequently done automobile service for the sheriff or his deputies, and taken a few miles north of the city, where a train was flagged, and thence carried to Bloomington, sixty miles north. A large number of persons in the crowd, not believing the Negroes had been taken away, demanded to go through the jail. The sheriff permitted them to select a committee of three, though they wanted seven, who about seven o'clock went through the jail. The mob was still unsatisfied and a half hour later three others were allowed to make the search. Those outside were still not satisfied but the sheriff then told them emphatically that he would not permit any more foolishness and he began clearing the streets about the jail. The members of Company C. and Troop D, I. N. G., who had begun assembling at the jail about 6:30 P.M. assisted the sheriff in dispersing the mob, firing two volleys over the heads of the crowd. The officers and soldiers were stoned by the rioters. Some of the crowd, among them the woman, Mrs. Kate Howard, who was later arrested, indicted for murder for participation in the lynching of Scott Burton, and who committed suicide on the way to the jail,—started the cry, "To Loper's"—Loper's being the restaurant owned by the man who had taken the Negroes away in his automobile.

About eight o'clock the mob reached Loper's restaurant. The obnoxious automobile was standing in front. The rioters demanded of Mr. Loper that he tell them where the Negroes were. This he refused to do, in spite of their threats. Then they broke in the front of the building with bricks and stones, upturned the automobile and set fire to it, and looted the place. The basement was used as a saloon, and they drank the liquors. I saw one group carrying off a tub of bottles of champagne; all were drinking from bottles. The money was stolen from the cash register, and even the silver and table linen were carried off, many of those arrested being found with the loot in their possession.

It took about three hours to wreck Loper's place. From there the now drunken mob went to East Washington Street, the "Levee," where it demolished and looted the Negro saloons and stores. One pawn shop was looted, on the pretext—purely fabricated,—that the owner had furnished fire arms to the Negroes, and here a number of revolvers were secured by the rioters who then went to the "bad lands" and began burning the houses of the Negroes. All the houses occupied by Negroes were burned from Ninth eastward to Twelfth street where Burton was hanged to a tree, after being shot, he having fired three shots at the mob from his door.

[Incidentally, two weeks later Mrs. Hallam confessed that her "attacker" was a white man whose identity she refused to divulge.]

The riot in Tulsa in 1921 began when a group of armed blacks prevented the lynching of a black porter accused of attempting to assault a white elevator girl. Less than a year earlier a mob had lynched a white man charged with murder. ["Sheriff Says Telephone Call Started Riot," *Tulsa Tribune*, June 3, 1921.]

A telephone call to a motion picture show in the black quarter was the first cause of the arming of the blacks, according to a statement made by Sheriff McCullough to Clark Betts, a staff correspondent of

St. Louis Post Dispatch and one of the out-of-town newspapermen here assigned to determine the causes of the battle.

"The telephone call came from some place in Tulsa proper," the sheriff said, "and it informed the negroes that an attempt was being made to lynch Rowland.

"Barney Cleaver and another negro officer called me up at once and asked me if they should come to the jail. I told them to stay in the black quarter and try to calm the negroes. Later they called me several times and finally I told Cleaver that he could slip over after while. He came over alone later.

At 4 o'clock Police Commissioner Adkison called me and told me there was some reports around the city of an attempt to lynch Rowland. Adkison said then that the safe thing to do would be to get the negro out of town. At that time I didn't know the negro was in the jail.

"There were no facts given me that the rumors had a basis and I didn't place much stock in them. I knew that I could protect the jail and that no mob could take a prisoner out of there. However, I stayed at the jail all evening and at 8:20 three men whom I did not know came into the corridor on the first floor of the courthouse. I went into the corridor and told them there had been some talk of a lynching and that they might as well get out for not one was going to get the negro. They went out and got into an auto on Boulder street. They sat there and talked loudly and gesticulated and soon a crowd gathered. Then I called all my white deputies and told them to run the elevator to the top of the building and to station themselves inside the jail and not to open the jail door under any circumstances. The mob could only gain access to the jail floor by going up a narrow stairway. The guards were behind the door at the top of the stairway.

"After this was done I went across the street and told the crowd to disperse. I was hooted and jeered but the auto in which the three men sat drove away. It returned soon, however, and the crowd kept growing. Not more than 100 of them could be termed members of a mob and I saw no weapons among the whites.

"An hour later 25 armed negroes marched to the court house down Sixth street. I met them and urged them to disperse, that the negro prisoner was safe and would not be taken out of the jail. They went away but returned shortly with many more armed blacks. Cleaver had appeared meanwhile. I disarmed two of the negroes quietly but did not order my deputies to disarm all of them because I thought that would have meant a general riot at that time. I thought I could get them into a frame of mind to leave. Just then a negro on the Sixth street side of the court house fired a shot.

"Instantly all the negroes began to fire into the air, running away

as they fired. Then the whites who were armed drew their guns and
I went back into the building. The race war was on and I was powerless to stop it. I took the negro prisoner away at 8 o'clock the next
morning."

The Reverend Harold G. Cooke, pastor of the Centenary Methodist
Church, told his congregation the story that came to be accepted by
white Tulsans. [From the *Tulsa Tribune,* June 6, 1921.]

"There has been a great deal of loose-mouthed and loose-minded
talking about the white people of Tulsa being equally to blame with
the blacks. This is not true. Any person that makes this assertion makes
an assertion that is false to the core. As an eye-witness of this tragedy
I want to state that there is only one thing that could have possibly
incited this tragedy and that was the appearance of armed negroes
in the white business section of Tulsa.

"The crowd of people gathered around the courthouse was not a
mob. It was largely, if not entirely a crowd of curious, unarmed and
innocent people, both men and women. Together with a friend I
moved among the crowd endeavoring to ascertain their motives and
intention, and I did not hear one single expression that signified the
spirit of mob violence. But when criminal and liquor-frenzied niggers
appeared on the streets and outraged the white people of this community, the thing was off."

Black Soldiers, White Police

The massive attacks on blacks in Memphis in 1866 began after a
sharp skirmish between black troops still stationed there and white
policemen. Whites believed these troops showed far too little respect,
and black troops believed the police used far too much force in making arrests. Dr. S. J. Quimby testifies. [From *Memphis Riots and
Massacres,* pp. 104–6.]

. . . The colored troops in the fort had been mustered out of service
and were waiting their payments. On Tuesday afternoon some hundred of them were out on a drunk; there was a grocery near my store
where they seemed to be getting most of their whiskey. There were,
I should judge, about fifty of them who were pretty drunk. Along in
the afternoon, about three o'clock, I heard up on Main street, which
is only about one block from where they were, great cheering. I

stepped out to inquire the cause; they said the officers had been up there arresting a man and the soldiers had rescued him. There was at that time no other fight. About four o'clock in the afternoon, perhaps an hour after this, while I was standing in my office-door there came by in the direction of Causey street six police officers; four of them stopped next door to me, and the other two went along to the crowd. There were two soldiers who were very boisterous in the crowd and the two officers arrested them, showing at the time no arms that I saw, but made the arrests in a perfectly orderly manner. As the police officers took the men along, the soldiers began to gather around them from all over the street, and began to call out, "Stone them, club them, shoot them," and all sorts of expressions that an excited body of men would use; they were all colored. The officers took the men and started down in the direction of Causey street; the other four officers joined in a little distance behind and attempted to keep the crowd off. Before they got to the first bayou, which is about fifty yards from my office, the soldiers began to fire their revolvers in the air; from what I saw I should judge there were about forty of them armed with revolvers, and the rest had stones, clubs, and whatever else they could get hold of. As they began firing in the air the officers seemed to think that they were firing at them, turned round and began firing at the crowd. Then, at once, I saw the crowd firing at them, and heard one of the crowd sing out, "One of them," meaning an officer, "was shot." I saw him carried into a grocery; then a part of the crowd went on and a part came back. In the course of some six or eight minutes I heard one of the colored soldiers speak back to the crowd, making the remark, "They have killed one of our men." At that all this crowd that had come back reloaded their revolvers, or took whatever they could get in their hands to fight with, and ran back towards the police, very much excited; they turned down Causey street, so that I saw no more of them until they came back. They returned in about a quarter of an hour, and remarked that they had killed one of the officers. I saw two soldiers come back who were wounded, and one of them had a policeman's club.

* * *

1142. Was it quiet all Tuesday night? Yes, with the exception of this crowd that came up from town. If it had not been for them, it would have been as quiet as it ever was. The police were there and their posse. This was after everything was through and the soldiers were all at the fort. There came up two hundred men, all armed. They patrolled up and down the street by fours, and when they found there were no soldiers there they scattered around in small squads and went among the [Negro] shanties, "hunting for arms," they said. They were breaking open houses, and killed four men that I knew.

During World War II, a riot erupted in Harlem after a white policeman shot a black soldier. [From "The Harlem Riot," *The Crisis* (September, 1943), L, 263.]

There were many sound, sensible editorial expressions on the Harlem riot from all sections of the country, but of the 346 daily newspaper editorials examined in this office, the one by the Richmond, Va., *Times Dispatch* easily ranks with the worst. To counteract the *Times Dispatch*, easily one of the best was from the neighboring Norfolk *Virginian-Pilot*. Louis I. Jaffe is still the scholarly and thoughtful editor of the Norfolk morning daily, while our old "friend," Virginius Dabney bosses the editorial page of the Richmond morning paper.

Dabney's diatribe entitled, "Dixie's Fault, Of Course," is unworthy of him even considering his obsession with the idea that northern Negro agitators are responsible for all the racial tension in the country. Dabney sneers at the idea that mistreatment of Negro soldiers in the South could have had anything whatsoever to do with sparking the riot of August 1–2 in far-away Harlem. It is this type of thinking which has made riots possible, this failure to realize that there is widespread knowledge and resentment of the general treatment of the race and particularly of the Negro soldier.

A soldier in uniform was shot by a policeman in Harlem. The question of who was right and who was wrong at the moment did not interest the mob. Mobs, white or black, don't reason. The white Beaumont mob did not reason. A white woman had not been raped, but you could not tell them that—not that night. So, in Harlem the wildfire story was of the shooting of a Negro soldier in uniform by a civilian policeman.

Negro soldiers have been shot down by civilian police in Alexandria, La., in Little Rock, Ark., in Baltimore, Md., in Beaumont, Texas, and in a half dozen other places. They have been humiliated, manhandled, and beaten in countless instances.

The Harlem mob knew all this. It hated all this. It could not reach the Arkansas cop who fired a full magazine of his revolver into the prone body of a Negro sergeant, or any of the others, so it tore up Harlem. It was a wild, senseless, criminal action, the boiling over of people who felt they could not get the Dabneys, the Connallys, or even the Roosevelts, much less the War department, the governors, the mayors, the chiefs of police to listen and act.

For his own purposes Dabney has caricatured the picture. Harlem's riot was not exclusively and solely the fault of Dixie. It was New York City's riot and New York City must bear its share of blame. All the old problems are there; and New York is a part of America, in many ways very like Dixie. But the stimulant in this particular instance did come from below the Mason and Dixon line; every Negro feels that in his bones, and white men, in Richmond as in New York, should understand it. In the minds of Harlemites that Sunday night the gun in the hands of a good New York policeman doing his duty was the gun in the hands of Dixie cops shooting down men in the uniform, if you please, of the Army of Democracy. That's the fact, much too big and much too bitter to be laughed away.

Mistaken Identity?

From the vantage point of history, sociologist Elliott Rudwick has attempted to piece together events surrounding the killing of two white policemen by blacks which touched off the riot at East St. Louis in 1917. [From Elliott M. Rudwick, *Race Riot at East St. Louis, July 2, 1917* (Carbondale: Southern Illinois University Press, 1964), pp. 36–40. Reprinted by permission of the publisher.]

On June 17 an embryonic race riot mob of several hundred whites threatened a sixty-six-year-old Negro who was then beaten into insensibility. According to the *Journal,* he "had refused to give his seat on a Collinsville streetcar to an elderly white lady." The following week other Negroes were attacked by white gangs, and the newspaper announced that "race rioting had resumed." It was no coincidence that these last assaults occurred just after the dwindling corps of pickets at the Aluminum Ore plant decided for "patriotic" motives to call off their strike. They had experienced two months of bitter frustration and defeat; their union, having failed to obtain recognition, stood impotent before the U.S. marshals and Illinois militiamen.

Despite the police having arrested none of the gangs of whites beating Negroes, Mayor Mollman later reported that colored people had "made no individual retaliations . . . to defend themselves." Time and again, when they went across the East St. Louis-St. Louis Free Bridge, they were "abused, hooted, and chased," and in late June a Negro committee complained to Mollman. This delegation, headed

by Dr. Le Roy Bundy and Dr. L. B. Bluitt, who was the assistant
county physician, prophetically told the Mayor there was a real danger
that a victim might kill one of the tormentors and plunge the city
into a disastrous race riot. Mollman expressed surprise and dismay,
indicating that he had judged race relations to be considerably improved since the first week of June. His remark was somewhat strange,
not only because of the repeated assaults, but also because during
the entire month East St. Louis whites circulated the rumor that
Negroes were arming to stage a July 4 massacre in revenge for the
May riots. The Negro variation of the same rumor was that the whites
intended to slaughter them on July 4.

*   *   *

The forebearance of East St. Louis Negroes ended four days after
that interview. Early on Sunday evening, July 1, several more white
assaults on Negroes were reported. About seven o'clock that night one
man was beaten and may have shot his white assailant. The incident,
like the others, occurred near Tenth and Bond Avenue. Between
nine and ten o'clock an hysterical colored woman in a torn dress told
a crowd of Negro men that whites had just beaten her and several
others at Eleventh and Trendley. Someone shouted, "Let's go to 10th
Street." However, several in the group advised them to return to
their homes.

Between ten-thirty and midnight, a Ford car (possibly two) driven
by whites fired shots into Negro homes along Market Street, near
Seventeenth. On a second foray, the residents were prepared and returned the fire, striking the automobile which disappeared in the night.
Although the police did nothing about the whites, they received a
report that armed Negroes were on a rampage. A Ford squad car
was dispatched immediately to make an investigation. In the front
seat of the police automobile were the driver and two detectives in
civilian clothes. Uniformed officers sat in back and a reporter for the
St. Louis *Republic*, Roy Albertson, stood on the running board. Early
the following morning, the *Republic* published the newsman's account
of the police encounter with the Negroes—without doubt this particular version helped to incite an East St. Louis population already on
the verge of riot.

According to Albertson, the police car turned into Bond Avenue
from Tenth, meeting "more than 200 rioting armed negroes . . . who
without a word of warning opened fire." Samuel Coppedge, one of the
detectives, was killed almost instantly and the other, Frank Wadley,
died the following day. Albertson wrote that the Negroes had pre-
arranged the murder. Other newspapers repeated this account of a

premeditated, unprovoked, and senseless killing. The assailants were portrayed as so calloused that they opened fire upon lawmen who had extended an offer of protection. Through this version, East St. Louisans were confirmed in their view that Negroes, stirred up by agitators and intoxicated by new Northern freedom, were the aggressors who had determined by any unlawful means to take control of the city.

In his article for the *Republic,* Albertson ommitted certain facts which, although not excusing the crime, certainly explained it. Testifying during the autumn of 1917 before the Congressional Committee investigating the riot, Albertson admitted that the murder could have been a case of mistaken identity.

Tenth and Bond Avenue was almost totally dark, a street light was at least fifty feet around the corner from where the Negroes were, and the headlights on the police car were "very poor." In his original articles on July 2 and 3, he had written that Detective Coppedge flashed his badge, identifying himself to the Negroes; but at the Congressional hearings Albertson was asked, "How could a policeman show his star to a man in the dark, with the automobile stopping and off again in a minute? What could the Negroes see about a star in the dark?" The reporter replied, "I don't know." Congressman John E. Raker suggested that the armed Negroes mistook the Ford police car for the Ford which white assailants had used to shoot into colored homes shortly before the lawmen had arrived:

> Now, as a matter of fact, if marauders had gone through those negro quarters and had shot into the houses and terrorized those people, the way the police car drove in front of those negroes that night, irrespective of whether they were armed or not—and in the dark, without being able to see who was in the machine—isn't it reasonable to suppose they thought there was another gang of marauders coming there to kill them as well as destroy their property. Isn't it reasonable?

Albertson admitted that it was indeed reasonable.

On the morning of July 2, Sergeant Coppedge's bullet-riddled car was parked before the police station in downtown East St. Louis. The Ford, with its blood-stained upholstery, "looked like a flour sieve, all punctured full of holes." Laborers on their way to work gathered around it, talking about getting revenge. A local attorney remarked that he would gladly act as counsel for "any man that would avenge the murders." The attack upon the detectives gave East St. Louisans "proof" they needed that Negro "armies" were mobilizing for a massacre, and in the face of that threat the whites were ready to wage a race war.

Civil Rights

In the general context of a garbage collector's strike, a civil rights
demonstration led by Martin Luther King, Jr., set off a wave of rioting
by blacks in Memphis in March of 1968. And when Dr. King returned
to Memphis the following week to prove he could hold a nonviolent
march, he was murdered by a white sniper. This murder touched off
riots in cities throughout the nation. ["Memphis: King's Biggest Gamble," by Robert M. Ratcliffe, *Pittsburgh Courier*, April 6, 1968.]

Martin Luther King took the big gamble here last Thursday, and
lost: his prestige went on a nosedive and his image was dented and
cracked.

Dr. King put his international fame on the line when he dared lead
10,000 or more on a march that was already out of hand before it
started.

First sign of trouble popped up when Memphis' handful of "black
power" youngsters and "the invaders" rushed to the front of the march
ahead of Dr. King. They refused to move back and shouted: "King
is not our leader, we want Carmichael."

Anticipating serious trouble, the Rev. James M. Lawson, Jr. of
Memphis, advised King to get into a car and move out of sight until
the "black power" group could be brought under control. It was
learned that Rev. Mr. Lawson would have called off the march if
given the necessary encouragement.

King's aides reportedly recommended that he go on with the march
through downtown Memphis, and off they marched.

What happened a few minutes later made international headlines.

The widely [*sic*] ballyhooed march, composed of thousands of junior
and senior high school students who had cut classes and hundreds of
adults who took a day off from work, was to have been a peaceful
one in behalf of 1,300 negro sanitation workers on strike nearly two
months.

The mass of humanity, taking up all street and sidewalk space,
moved off around 11 a.m. from in front of historic Clayborn Temple
AME Church, up Hernando to famed Beale St. and then west on
Beale to Main St.

Smashing of store windows and looting began on Beale just as
march leaders turned into Main St., and there was more window-
smashing and looting for one block on Main St.

It was at this point that Dr. King and local march leaders agreed that the thing was out of hand. The more than 600 policemen on duty were called into action. Tear gas was squirted into faces of flee-ing marchers, many of the looters, and those who couldn't run fast enough, were beaten with police sticks.

["The Legacy of Dr. King," by Robert E. Baskin, *Dallas Morning News*, April 10, 1968. Selections from the *Dallas Morning News* are reprinted by permission of the publisher.]

The senseless slaying of Dr. Martin Luther King in Memphis has left this capital and much of the nation benumbed and devastatingly saddened.

But in the wake of the assassination there are strange and troubling sights on the American scene that do not speak well for politicians, the Negro militants or the nation's society as a whole.

The fabric of our civilization has been harshly torn in Washington, Detroit, Chicago and a host of other cities as lawlessness has reigned in an atmosphere of flames, looting and violence.

All of this was triggered by the death of Dr. King.

But anyone who saw the mobs at work in Washington last weekend quickly realized that they were not memorializing him.

Indeed—if emotions could be set aside in evaluating the situation—one could only conclude that they were hard at work repudiating the non-violence he preached.

Their activities, instead of enhancing the memory of Dr. King were demonstrating that his policies, by and large, had served in recent years mainly to promote violence in his wake.

In Memphis only a week before his death a peaceful march led by Dr. King had set off vicious rioting which seemed to surprise and frighten him. But he went right ahead with plans for a spring and summer of demonstrations that surely could have led only to more divisiveness and strife over the country.

Recreation and Fist Fights

Sunday afternoon battles between black and white teenagers over the use of recreation facilities erupted into serious black-white riots in Chicago in 1919 and Detroit in 1943. [From Chicago Commission on Race Relations, *The Negro in Chicago*, pp. 4–5.]

It was four o'clock Sunday afternoon, July 27, when Eugene Wil-liams, seventeen-year-old Negro boy, was swimming offshore at the foot of Twenty-ninth Street. This beach was not one of those publicly maintained and supervised for bathing, but it was much used. Although it flanks an area thickly inhabited by Negroes, it was used by both races, access being had by crossing the railway tracks which skirt the lake shore. The part near Twenty-seventh Street had by tacit understanding come to be considered as reserved for Negroes, while the whites used the part near Twenty-ninth Street. Walking is not easy along the shore, and each race had kept pretty much to its own part, observing, moreover, an imaginary boundary extending into the water.

Williams, who had entered the water at the part used by Negroes, swam and drifted south into the part used by the whites. Immediately before his appearance there, white men, women, and children had been bathing in the vicinity and were on the beach in considerable numbers. Four Negroes walked through the group and into the water. White men summarily ordered them off. The Negroes left, and the white people resumed their sport. But it was not long before the Negroes were back, coming from the north with others of their race. Then began a series of attacks and retreats, counter-attacks, and stone-throwing. Women and children who could not escape hid behind debris and rocks. The stone-throwing continued, first one side gaining the advantage, then the other.

Williams, who had remained in the water during the fracas, found a railroad tie and clung to it, stones meanwhile frequently striking the water near him. A white boy of about the same age swam toward him. As the white boy neared, Williams let go of the tie, took a few strokes, and went down. The coroner's jury rendered a verdict that he had drowned because fear of stone-throwing kept him from shore. His body showed no stone bruises, but rumor had it that he had actually been hit by one of the stones and drowned as a result.

On shore guilt was immediately placed upon a certain white man by several Negro witnesses who demanded that he be arrested by a white policeman who was on the spot. No arrest was made.

The tragedy was sensed by the battling crowd and, awed by it, they gathered on the beach. For an hour both whites and Negroes dived for the boy without results. Awe gave way to excited whispers. "They" said he was stoned to death. The report circulated through the crowd that the police officer had refused to arrest the murderer. The Negroes in the crowd began to mass dangerously. At this crucial point the accused policeman arrested a Negro on a white man's complaint. Negroes mobbed the white officer and the riot was under way.

*   *   *

The two facts, the drowning and the refusal to arrest, or widely circulated reports of such refusal, must be considered together as marking the inception of the riot. Testimony of a captain of police shows that first reports from the lake after the drowning indicated that the situation was calming down. White men had shown a not altogether hostile feeling for the Negroes by assisting in diving for the body of the boy. Furthermore a clash started on this isolated spot could not be augmented by outsiders rushing in. There was every possibility that the clash, without the further stimulus of reports of the policeman's conduct, would have quieted down.

Chronological story of the riot. After the drowning of Williams, it was two hours before any further fatalities occurred. Reports of the drowning and of the alleged conduct of the policeman spread out into the neighborhood. The Negro crowd from the beach gathered at the foot of Twenty-ninth Street. As it became more and more excited, a group of officers was called by the policeman who had been at the beach. James Crawford, a Negro, fired into the group of officers and was himself shot and killed by a Negro policeman who had been sent to help restore order.

During the remainder of the afternoon of July 27, many distorted rumors circulated swiftly throughout the South Side. The Negro crowd from Twenty-ninth Street got into action, and white men who came in contact with it were beaten. In all, four white men were beaten, five were stabbed, and one was shot. As the rumors spread, new crowds gathered, mobs sprang into activity spontaneously, and gangs began to take part in the lawlessness.

Farther to the west, as darkness came on, white gangsters became active. Negroes in white districts suffered severely at their hands. From 9:00 P.M. until 3:00 A.M. twenty-seven Negroes were beaten, seven were stabbed, and four were shot.

Governor Kelly of Michigan appointed a fact-finding body consisting of the state attorney general, prosecuting attorney, police commissioner, and the Detroit police commissioner. Its "Factual Report" (called the Dowling Report, after Prosecuting Attorney William E. Dowling) seemed intent on assigning full responsibility for the riot to unruly blacks and affirming the right conduct of all levels of law enforcement personnel. Its version of the sparking incident follows. [From Rushton, Dowling, Olander, and Witherspoon, "Factual Report," 1943. Part I, "Factual Statement of Incidents of June 20 & June 21."]

Belle Isle Park, Detroit's principal recreational center, is located in the Detroit River and is connected with the mainland by a large bridge at the intersection of E. Grand Boulevard and Jefferson Avenue. The Detroit Street Railway system furnishes bus transportation to the island. Recreational facilities provided at the island include picnic grounds, swimming beaches, swings, playgrounds, refreshment stands, and the customary pavilions. The park has long been famous because of its size, natural beauty, and its many recreational facilities. On that warm Sunday afternoon and evening, June 20, there were nearly 100,000 people on the Isle, the majority of whom were Negroes.

❋ ❋ ❋

The incidents occurring on Belle Isle were little different in character than those which had occurred elsewhere in and about Detroit for some time preceding June 20. On June 15, only five days before, there had been a disturbance at Eastwood Park, an amusement center located in Macomb County, just outside Detroit. On that occasion a group of colored boys was met by a stone attack by a number of white youths as the former were about to leave a street car in front of the park. The white boys prevented the colored youths from entering the park.

❋ ❋ ❋

Aaron Fox, colored, 17, went to Belle Isle with Raymond Thomas, 17, colored, on Sunday noon, June 20. Fox intended to go swimming, but the line waiting admission was too long. He spent considerable time wandering about the island. Later in the day these boys met Frank and Fred Neal, twins, 17, colored, and Kelly Lately, 14, colored, who had gone to the Isle with LeRoy Howell, 13, colored, at 3:30 in the afternoon. These six boys wandered to the playground where a number of colored youths were shooting dice. There they met Charles (Little Willie) Lyons, 20, colored, who had come to the island with H. D. (Handsome Harry) Minnifield, 17, colored. Aaron Fox and Charles Lyons talked of the Eastwood Park episode in which they had been involved. They agreed it would be a good idea to: "Go fight and do like they done us at Eastwood Park." Lyons suggested to the crowd of colored boys there at the playground that they: "Take care of the Hunkies." At the time there were several white people using the swings at the playground. The first incident occurred when Lyons, arming himself with a stick wrapped in paper, approached a white boy, struck him, and ordered him to leave the island. The white boy ran. There were at the time several white men seated on the grass. Lyons struck the feet of one of these white men, telling him: "Time to go home. Get going." The white men left. This colored group then began canvassing the island for white boys.

❋ ❋ ❋

The crowd of Negroes, including Mattie Mae (Redcap) Byndon, had continued in the meantime toward the Jefferson Avenue terminus of the bridge. Eleanor Giusto, white, her sister, Stella Redko, 18, and Margaret Hart, 17, attracted by the excitement, had started across the bridge. They were met by three white sailors who informed them that there had been trouble between whites and Negroes at the swings on the playground. One of the sailors told the girls that a colored man had been involved in a fight with a white sailor and his girl-friend, and that the Negro had cut the white sailor. After talking for a few minutes, the girls decided to return to Jefferson Avenue. There was momentary quiet until the Byndon girl, walking with her friends, pushed against Eleanor Giusto. The Negress says that Margaret Hart called her a "black bitch," which provoked her to exclaim: "You mother-fucking bastard," and to strike Miss Hart. Margaret Hart denies the statement, but admits returning the blow, striking Miss Byndon with her fist. The colored boys with the Negress attacked Miss Hart, knocking her down and kicking her. This colored group then ran to Jefferson Avenue, the three sailors who had spoken to the girls remaining aloof from the disturbance. Suddenly, Stella Redko heard a scream coming from the bushes near the approach to the bridge. A crowd of white people ran toward the bushes. Separate fights broke out the length of the bridge and along Jefferson Avenue.

When Aaron Fox reached Jefferson Avenue, he suggested to the crowd that they return to Belle Isle. He told them that a colored woman and her baby had been drowned. Police reinforcements had arrived, however, and this group of boys refused to go back.

Meantime, the traffic leading from Belle Isle was heavy, and crowds of people were in and about the intersection of E. Jefferson and E. Grand Boulevard, and there was heavy traffic on those two arteries. Numerous whites returning home via E. Jefferson Avenue stopped, many joining in the mellee that had developed. The Negroes at the bridge approach were at the time outnumbered by whites. By 11:20 p.m., the crowd at the bridge approach had increased to more than 5,000, and the street fighting had spread west to Helen Avenue, east to Field, and north to Lafayette East.

❖   ❖   ❖

The police in the meantime had blocked off the Belle Isle approach, preventing anyone entering the island. By 2 o'clock in the morning of June 21, the augmented police force had succeeded, without firing a single shot, in dispersing the crowds and placing the situation under complete control. The casualties resulting from disturbances at Belle Isle and the bridge approach from eight o'clock in the evening of June 20, until 2 o'clock the following morning numbered 13, of which

8 were white and 5 were colored. There were no riot casualties in the Fifth Precinct after that hour. None of the casualties occurring in this area, resulting from the initial disturbance, was serious. There is no record of the use of any firearms by any trouble makers during this period in this area. Weapons employed by either whites or Negroes there were stones, sticks and knives.

Had the disturbance ended with the incidents at Belle Isle and the bridge approach, none of the deaths occurring in the riot would have resulted. More than 98% of the injuries would have been avoided; upwards of 95% of the reported property damage resulting from the rioting would never have been suffered; less than 3% of the reported law violations would have existed; less than 3% of the arrests made incident to the rioting would have been made.

But rioting was started by an episode which occurred at the Forest Club, 700 E. Forest, in the heart of the Negro section some five miles from Belle Isle. This occurrence excited passions and must be cited as the principal cause of the tragedy which followed.

The Forest Club is one of the larger recreational centers located in the Negro section of Detroit, commonly referred to as Paradise Valley. The club consists of a dance hall, a roller skating rink, and a bowling alley at the above address. Patrons, all Negroes, estimated at 700 in number, attended a dance there on Sunday evening, June 20. Shortly after midnight, Leo Tipton, an employee of the Forest Club Ballroom, assigned to the checkroom that night, appeared on the stage, and seizing the microphone in front of the orchestra leader, aroused the dancers with the following announcement: "This is Sergeant Fuller [a Negro police officer]. There's a riot at Belle Isle. The whites have killed a colored lady and baby. Thrown them over the bridge. Everybody get their hat and coat and come on. There is free transportation outside." Pandemonium broke loose! Some of the dancers dashed out of the building; others jumped out of the windows. Tamble Whitworth, a special officer working at the ballroom, attempted to dissuade the people from leaving, but to no avail. The crowd milled about the intersection of E. Forest and Hasting Streets. The transportation Leo Tipton had announced was available was not there to transport all of the mob. Automobiles operated by whites, stopping at the traffic signal at the intersection, were opened by members of the Negro mob, the whites taken from behind the wheel, and the vehicle appropriated.

Simultaneously, the crowd commenced to throw stones at the passing vehicles and street cars. A white motorcyclist traveling east on Forest was struck by a stone. He fell off the motorcycle. Another stone struck the motor causing gasoline to spurt, setting fire to the

cycle. At about 12:10 a.m., Tamble Whitworth called the police re-
porting the first rioting outside the Belle Isle area.

Arrests During Long Hot Summers

In the 1960s, black riots have erupted during hot summers when
opportunities for clashes with police are greatest and mobs most likely
to collect around fairly common incidents. Each riot has had its particular spark, usually something like the following. [The following
selections are from the Kerner Report, pp. 22–23; the McCone Report, pp. 10–12; and "Detroit's Time of Trouble: It Began with a
Raid Here . . ." by William Serrin, in the *Detroit Free Press* (August
6, 1967). Selections from the *Detroit Free Press* are reprinted by permission of the publisher.]

Tampa, 1967

On Sunday, June 11, 1967, Tampa, Fla., sweltered in the 94-degree
heat. A humid wind ruffled the bay, where thousands of persons
watched the hydroplane races. Since early morning the Police Department's Selective Enforcement Unit, designed as a riot control squad,
had been employed to keep order at the races.

At 5:30 P.M., a block from the waterfront, a photo supply ware-
house was broken into. Forty-five minutes later two police officers
spotted three Negro youths as they walked near the State Building.
When the youths caught sight of the officers, they ducked into an
alley. The officers gave chase. As they ran, the suspects left a trail of
photographic equipment scattered from yellow paper bags they were
carrying.

The officers transmitted a general broadcast over the police radio.
As other officers arrived on the scene, a chase began through and
around the streets, houses, and alleys of the neighborhood. When
Negro residents of the area adjacent to the Central Park Village
Housing Project became aware of the chase, they began to participate.
Some attempted to help the officers in locating the suspects.

R. C. Oates, one of 17 Negroes on the 511-man Tampa police force,
spotted 19-year-old Martin Chambers, bare to the waist, wriggling
away beneath one of the houses. Oates called for Chambers to surrender. Ignoring him, Chambers emerged running from beneath the
house. A white officer, J. L. Calvert, took up the pursuit.

Pursuing Calvert, in turn, were three young Negroes, all spectators.

Behind one of the houses a high cyclone fence created a 2-foot wide alley 25 feet in length.

As Chambers darted along the fence, Officer Calvert rounded the corner of the house. Calvert yelled to him to halt. Chambers ignored him. Calvert pointed his .38 revolver and fired. The slug entered the back of Chambers and passed completely through his body. Raising his hands over his head, he clutched at the cyclone fence.

When the three youths running behind Officer Calvert came upon the scene, they assumed Chambers had been shot standing in the position in which they saw him. Rumor quickly spread through the neighborhood that a white police officer had shot a Negro youth who had had his hands over his head and was trying to surrender.

The ambulance that had been summoned became lost on the way. The gathering crowd viewing the bloody, critically injured youth grew increasingly belligerent.

Los Angeles, 1965

On August 11, 1965, California Highway Patrolman Lee W. Minikus, a Caucasian, was riding his motorcycle along 122nd street, just south of the Los Angeles City boundary, when a passing Negro motorist told him he had just seen a car that was being driven recklessly. Minikus gave chase and pulled the car over at 116th and Avalon, in a predominantly Negro neighborhood, near but not in Watts. It was 7:00 p.m.

The driver was Marquette Frye, a 21-year-old Negro, and his older brother, Ronald, 22, was a passenger. Minikus asked Marquette to get out and take the standard Highway Patrol sobriety test. Frye failed the test, and at 7:05 p.m. Minikus told him he was under arrest. He radioed for his motorcycle partner, for a car to take Marquette to jail, and a tow truck to take the car away.

They were two blocks from the Frye home, in an area of two-story apartment buildings and numerous small family residences. Because it was a very warm evening, many of the residents were outside.

Ronald Frye, having been told he could not take the car when Marquette was taken to jail, went to get their mother so that she could claim the car. They returned to the scene about 7:15 p.m. as the second motorcycle patrolman, the patrol car, and tow truck arrived. The original group of 25 to 50 curious spectators had grown to 250 to 300 persons.

Mrs. Frye approached Marquette and scolded him for drinking. Marquette, who until then had been peaceful and cooperative, pushed her away and moved toward the crowd, cursing and shouting at the officers that they would have to kill him to take him to jail. The patrolmen pursued Marquette and he resisted.

The watching crowd became hostile, and one of the patrolmen radioed for more help. Within minutes, three more highway patrolmen arrived. Minikus and his partner were now struggling with both Frye brothers. Mrs. Frye, now belligerent, jumped on the back of one of the officers and ripped his shirt. In an attempt to subdue Marquette, one officer swung at his shoulder with a night stick, missed, and struck him on the forehead, inflicting a minor cut. By 7:23 p.m., all three of the Fryes were under arrest, and other California Highway Patrolmen and, for the first time, Los Angeles police officers had arrived in response to the call for help.

Officers on the scene said there were now more than 1,000 persons in the crowd. About 7:25 p.m., the patrol car with the prisoners, and the tow truck pulling the Frye car, left the scene. At 7:31 p.m., the Fryes arrived at a nearby sheriff's substation.

Undoubtedly the situation at the scene of the arrest was tense. Belligerence and resistance to arrest called for forceful action by the officers. This brought on hostility from Mrs. Frye and some of the bystanders, which, in turn, caused increased actions by the police. Anger at the scene escalated and, as in all such situations, bitter recriminations from both sides followed.

Considering the undisputed facts, the Commission finds that the arrest of the Fryes was handled efficiently and expeditiously. The sobriety test administered by the California Highway Patrol and its use of a transportation vehicle for the prisoner and a tow truck to remove his car are in accordance with the practices of other law enforcement agencies, including the Los Angeles Police Department.

The Spitting Incident. As the officers were leaving the scene, someone in the crowd spat on one of them. They stopped withdrawing and two highway patrolmen went into the crowd and arrested a young Negro woman and a man who was said to have been inciting the crowd to violence when the officers were arresting her. Although the wisdom of stopping the withdrawal to make these arrests has been questioned, the Commission finds no basis for criticizing the judgment of the officers on the scene.

Following these arrests, all officers withdrew at 7:40 p.m. As the last police car left the scene, it was stoned by the now irate mob.

As has happened so frequently in riots in other cities, inflated and distorted rumors concerning the arrests spread quickly to adjacent areas. The young woman arrested for spitting was wearing a barber's smock, and the false rumor spread throughout the area that she was pregnant and had been abused by police. Erroneous reports were

also circulated concerning the treatment of the Fryes at the arrest
scene.

The crowd did not disperse, but ranged in small groups up and
down the street, although never more than a few blocks from the arrest
scene. Between 8:15 p.m. and midnight, the mob stoned automobiles,
pulled Caucasian motorists out of their cars and beat them, and
menaced a police field command post which had been set up in the
area. By 1:00 a.m., the outbreak seemed to be under control, but until
early morning hours, there were sporadic reports of unruly mobs, vandalism, and rock throwing. Twenty-nine persons were arrested.

Detroit, 1967

Meet William Scott. Call him Bill.

He doesn't look like a bad guy. He is really a regular fellow, easy
come, easy go.

He even likes to toss a party now and then, and it was just two
weeks ago Sunday that he threw his last one. A couple of servicemen
friends were back from Vietnam, and another was maybe going to go.
And if there's one thing Bill Scott likes to do, it's be friendly to the
men in uniform.

At least, Scott calls the shindig a party. The police say otherwise.
They say Bill Scott is actually a businessman, and was working late.
They say he was running a blind pig [an illegal, all-night saloon].

Be that as it may, about 3:45 a.m. that Sunday, Patrolman Charles
Henry, a Negro in plainclothes, gained admittance to Scott's party
and obtained a beer.

Scott says it was on the house. Henry says he paid 50 cents.

Ten minutes later, officers from the Tenth Precinct, led by Sgt.
Arthur Howison, a putty-faced pro, raided the party, upstairs in the
old Economy Printing Co., at 9125 Twelfth St.

The 50 cents was supposed to be the raid's only cost. It wasn't.

Before the next five days had ended, the raid had cost the city at
least 41 dead, more than $250 million in property damage and an
estimated $10.5 million to the city in extra costs and lost revenue.

The wisdom of the raid is, of course, suspect in light of the climate
of Negro violence that had been sweeping the country and the fact
that Twelfth St. is one of the most volatile Negro streets in Detroit.

Still, Howison could no doubt have pulled it off without incident,
had it not been for two circumstances: It was an exceedingly hot,
muggy night, and perhaps the worst of the year, and the Negroes on
Twelfth St. really had their thirsts up, and had jammed the hall far
in excess of Howison's estimates.

The last time Howison had raided the place, in August, 1966, he had picked up 14 revelers. This time, he found 85.

He was dumbfounded. He picked up a telephone and called for two more paddy wagons to join the one parked outside.

Scott was also up in the air. It was unconstitutional, he said, the fuzz crashing his little get-together.

It is fruitless to hit a speak-easy unless it can be proved that alcohol is being sold illegally. The accepted way of providing the proof is to make a plant: Slip a ringer, and have him buy a drink.

Getting a ringer into Scott's parties had always been difficult.

Howison had tried it at least five times before, but was always unsuccessful. This time, Henry had been forced to show real professionalism to complete his mission.

He had already been turned away from the party about 10:30 p.m. He had walked up to a doorman with fellow Patrolman Joseph Brown, also a Negro in plainclothes, and said that Brown was a basketball player from Cincinnati looking for some action. The doorman told them to split.

But about 3:45 (Henry and Brown had spent the intervening hours unsuccessfully trying to gain admittance to other Twelfth St. speaks) Henry spotted three Negro females, all bent on wetting their whistles. He joined up, and the four got through the doorman.

They walked up to the second floor. A peephole was opened and an eye surveyed them. They were passed again, so easily, in fact, that the second doorman didn't even ask Henry for the membership card in the United Civic League for Community Action that Howison had provided.

The raid came exactly in accordance with Tenth Precinct standard operating procedures: If the plant doesn't come out in 10 minutes, it's assumed the purchase has been made.

Howison and three men stormed the building, giving no stories about basketball players from Cincinnati. They broke the glass in the downstairs door, charged up the stairs and broke open the second door with a sledgehammer.

According to Scott and Mrs. Bernice Jones, a fellow Civic League official, it was all like a George Raft Prohibition movie on late TV.

"We heard these noises," Mrs. Jones said—"Pow, pow, pow. We thought it was gunshots (it apparently was the sledgehammer). Then we heard glass breaking. Then somebody shouted: 'It's a raid.'"

Scott adds: "Everybody was cowed. You couldn't hardly move for everybody getting under the tables."

Then, according to Scott and Mrs. Jones, some police guarded the front door while others nailed up two doors, in the rear.

Then Howison's reinforcements arrived and the 85 persons were hauled to the Tenth Precinct, on Livernois.

As it turned out, only three were charged: . . . All were cited for violation of state liquor laws.

The 82 persons arrested as loiterers were set free.

For three arrests, the raid may have been the most expensive pinch in history.

❀　　❀　　❀

Looking back, Howison says he has no second guesses about his action. Under the same circumstances, he says, he'd pull it off again.

He says it was conducted neither for spite, nor for the exercise. It was just another pig, he says. It needed knocking, so he knocked it.

Economy Printing is a landmark now, a genuine American curio, even if no plans have been made to move it to Greenfield Village.

"Yeah," said a National Guardsman one day last week, M-1 over one shoulder, transistor radio in his hand: "That's where it all started."

☞ 6 ☜

THE EXPLOSION

Once the match has been struck, the powder keg explodes, and its released forces are uncontrollable. Members of its mobs may offer long-standing fears or grievances or the need for immediate vengeance to justify their conduct, but the actual destruction of people and property suggests rampant bestiality. Based on the color of rioters, these explosions are of three types: white, white-black, and black.

A white riot is simply a massacre. New York City (1863), Memphis (1866), Atlanta (1906), Springfield (1908), East St. Louis (1917), and to a large extent Tulsa (1921), fit this category. Whites may label them "Negro uprisings" despite the fact that, in the words of U.S. Army General Stoneman in Memphis, 1866, after the initial conflict "the negroes had nothing to do with the riot, except to be killed and abused." Whites chase blacks who chance to be near, raid streetcars, hunt out places where black porters, waiters, or bootblacks are likely to be, and generally attack blacks indiscriminately and viciously. White men invade the black ghetto, burn houses and business establishments, and sometimes set fire to buildings in order to flush out and shoot blacks who have taken refuge inside. This is the only type of riot in which this kind of invasion occurs. The local law enforcement agents are usually ineffective: in New York City (1863) police did not hesitate to shoot and club rioters, but were overmatched; in other cases, however, police aid and abet the riot or at best turn their backs. Outside troops help restore order. Police and troops often are reluctant to use force against whites; they would rather arrest all blacks found carrying arms and herd as many blacks as possible out of the way.

Whether black or white strikes the first blow, both blacks and whites kill during a white-black riot. Sometimes blacks arm and defend themselves during a white riot. But in a white-black riot, of which Chicago (1919) and Detroit (1943) are the prime examples, the explosion is a series of battles. Gangs or mobs of one race assault isolated groups or individuals of the other, so that while black casualties are greater than white, the balance is closer than in the white riot. Whites own more property in black areas than do blacks in white areas; hence, they are more vulnerable to property destruction, while blacks are more vulnerable to personal assaults. Police show partiality toward white rioters admonishing them and shooting black rioters. The importation of outside troops, more nearly neutral in behavior and better prepared to impose order, provides the occasion for abandoning hostilities.

Black riots, except for those in Harlem (1935 and 1943) and Houston (1917), are a phenomenon of the 1960s and are confined to the black ghettos. Because of the massive segregation of the ghetto, there is little contact between black rioters and white civilians. The chief target is property, especially white-owned retail stores, which are looted and burned. But destruction, particularly by arson, soon becomes indiscriminate and general devastation follows. Those killed are chiefly blacks, almost all shot by law enforcement officers. The police, subject to harassment and some shooting, make massive arrests and play the role of beleaguered invaders in hostile territory; they are most active in this type of riot. Outside forces called in help quell the riots by forcing black people off the streets.

In general, the white riot came first in time, and the white-black succeeded it. Except for the kind of outbursts which occasionally result when black demonstrators clash with white hecklers, neither of these types has occurred since World War II. At first fearfully defending themselves against white assaults, blacks have gradually assumed the role of primary rioters, in a logical progression that moves from Memphis in 1866 (no defense) to Atlanta (minimal defense) to Washington (some defense after several days) to Tulsa (strong defense from the beginning) to Detroit in 1943 (substantial participation) to Watts in 1965 (a black production). This progression relates to the massing of blacks in urban ghettoes discussed in Chapter Three, continuation of the caste system despite greater efforts to reduce prejudice and segregation, the widening of the differential between black and white standards of living despite the increase in both, and the decreasing acceptance of social, political, and economic inferiority by blacks.

In all three types of riots a minority of the residents participates. Yet it is a significant minority. While most members of mobs may be passive, they inhibit law enforcement and prolong the actual strife. Most of the victims are innocent unfortunates who happened to be in the wrong spot. Whites nailed white cloths to their homes in Springfield and placed "No Colored Work Here" signs in business places in New York City; blacks scrawled "Soul Brother" on their stores in the riot areas during the 1960s. But because destruction ceases to be focused on retaliation, luck preserves more buildings than this attempt to invoke the "passover" technique, and efforts by residents to dissuade rioters have little impact once the match has flared. Finally, a combination of exhaustion and overwhelming force quenches the explosion.

Cooler Heads Do Not Prevail

The following selections show early attempts to prevent ugly situations from exploding. The mayor of Atlanta, civil rights leaders in Newark, a plainclothes policeman who was a major in the Oklahoma National Guard in Tulsa, and United States Representative John Conyers, a Negro, all failed to defuse the powder keg. [The first selection is from the *Atlanta Constitution*, September 23, 1906.]

Atlanta, July 22, 1906

During the early part of the night, while the reports of the assaults and attempted assaults on Atlanta women were being circulated around among the gathering crowds, being greatly exaggerated every minute, one of the largest of these assemblages was on North Pryor street, near Decatur street.

Even at this time the crowd was in the ugliest kind of a mood, and the cooler minds realized that trouble was brewing. A negro entered Casey's pool room. One man in the crowd insisted that the man was a bad nigger, and ought to be lynched. A rush was made to secure the negro from the place, the crowd growing uglier and uglier every minute.

It was at this stage of the proceedings that Mayor James Woodward, hat in hand, begged the crowd to remain quiet, and not to do anything that would bring shame to the city of which they were all so justly and pardonably proud.

"For God's sake, men," begged the mayor, "go to your homes quietly, and leave this matter in the hands of the law. I promise you that every negro will receive justice, and the guilty shall not escape. I beseech you not to cause this blot on the fair name of our most beautiful city. What you may do in a few minutes of recklessness will take Atlanta many years to recover from. I implore you to leave this matter in the hands of the law, and save the bloodshed that is sure to follow if you allow yourselves to be governed by these reports, that are certainly exaggerated."

Newark, July 13, 1967

[From the Kerner Report, pp. 34–35.]

Reports and rumors, including one that Smith had died [Editor's note: John Smith, a black cabdriver, whose arrest and detention had spawned rumors and sparked a confrontation between black citizens and Newark's Fourth Precinct police. In the course of arresting him for "tailgating" a squad car, policemen had administered a rather severe beating, which they insisted had been necessary to overcome his resistance.], circulated through the Negro community. Tension continued to rise. Nowhere was the tension greater than at the Spirit House, the gathering place for Black Nationalists, Black Power advocates, and militants of every hue. Black Muslims, Orthodox Muslims, and members of the United Afro-American Association, a new and growing organization that follows, in general, the teachings of the late Malcolm X, came regularly to mingle and exchange views. Anti-white playwright LeRoi Jones held workshops. The two police-Negro clashes, coming one on top of the other, coupled with the unresolved political issues, had created a state of crisis.

On Thursday, inflammatory leaflets were circulated in the neighborhoods of the Fourth Precinct. A "Police Brutality Protest Rally" was announced for early evening in front of the Fourth Precinct Station. Several television stations and newspapers sent news teams to interview people. Cameras were set up. A crowd gathered.

A picket line was formed to march in front of the police station. Between 7:00 and 7:30 P.M. James Threatt, Executive Director of the Newark Human Rights Commission, arrived to announce to the people the decision of the mayor to form a citizens group to investigate the Smith incident, and to elevate a Negro to the rank of captain.

The response from the loosely milling mass of people was derisive. One youngster shouted "Black Power!" Rocks were thrown at Threatt, a Negro. The barrage of missiles that followed placed the police station under siege.

After the barrage had continued for some minutes, police came out to disperse the crowd. According to witnesses, there was little restraint of language or action by either side. A number of police officers and Negroes were injured.

As on the night before, once the people had been dispersed, reports of looting began to come in. Soon the glow of the first fire was seen.

Without enough men to establish control, the police set a perimeter around a two-mile stretch of Springfield Avenue, one of the principal business districts, where bands of youths roamed up and down smashing windows. Grocery and liquor stores, clothing and furniture stores, drugstores and cleaners, appliance stores and pawnshops were the principal targets. Periodically, police officers would appear and fire their weapons over the heads of looters and rioters. Laden with stolen goods, people began returning to the housing projects.

Tulsa, May 31, 1921

[From the *Tulsa Tribune*, June 5, 1921.]

"I went down to the station about daylight in the morning," said Daley yesterday. "Col. Rooney and I had been out to the edge of town and to the Midland Valley stations looking for parties of negroes supposed to be entering the city. I had previously placed a pyramid line of volunteer guards at the Frisco to keep the crowd out of the Greenwood area. When I got back there I found it submerged in the crowd and out of control. The leaders of the mob were egging them to start burning and shooting and they were just about ready to cut loose when I stopped them. I told them to go back home and stay out of the streets. None of them knew I was a National Guard officer or even a policeman, so they started to threaten me. So I drew my gun and told them I would shoot the first man that crossed a line which I drew on the platform.

"Then I sent call after call to the police station for help. But everyone was out on the hills or in the other parts of town protecting people or conveying the negroes into camp. For about an hour and a half I stood there and argued and threatened with that mob, while some of the leaders kept pushing 'em on.

"They finally drew their guns on me from one side and I had to crack one fellow hard to keep him back. The crowd kept getting larger and larger, until finally the mob burst past me and ran for the business blocks across the tracks. I ran with them trying to hold them back but it was no use, so I went back to the station to get some more officers."

Detroit, July 23, 1967

[From Andrew Mollison, "The First Hours of the Riot: Why the Peacemakers Failed," *Detroit Free Press*, August 6, 1967.]

Police formed at Taylor, Hazelwood, Gladstone, Euclid and Philadelphia, apparently preparing to clear off Twelfth St.

Jovial taunts, obscene only because the Twelfth St. vernacular is obscene, were hurled. But a rock or two was thrown. A brick, a bottle.

One bottle-tosser hit the front window of a new laundromat at Taylor and Twelfth. Within two or three minutes another missile—some think a woman's pocketbook—smashed a window six blocks away at Euclid.

The sound of tinkling glass was too tempting.

"People who don't—I did not say wouldn't—ordinarily steal, respectable people, began it. The have nots joined in," said the Rev. Saunders.

Twelfth St. quickly became an eight-block long supermarket with no check-out counters.

Two boys about 14 struggled across the street with a hi-fi set. The crowd cheered them. "It was like I just hit a home run," one said later.

*   *   *

Conyers waded into the crowd that had gathered to watch the riot squad.

"We're not going to solve the problems of Twelfth St. in 15 minutes," he said, but he tried to talk people into leaving.

"Hey, baby, they don't live here. This ain't their home," a bystander said of the riot squad.

Conyers told the sergeant quietly: "This is provocative. Those bayonets."

The sergeant reminded Conyers that the squad had orders to be there. He said that a police pull-out in Watts, under similar circumstances, had led to increased violence.

Conyers returned to Grace Episcopal.

Locke still wasn't back with the bullhorns.

The group discussed the riot squad. The "hard-firm" men epitomized by Vance called for State Police and National Guard intervention. The "cool-firm" men epitomized by Witherspoon called for removal of the riot squad.

A new arrival, Arthur Johnson, assistant superintendent of schools, said:

"I think the situation can deteriorate with a show of force. People now are going to get mad and the bayonets are provocative."

The two TAP women brought coffee.

"Frankly, there's going to be some looting, but we'd better have that rather than a war between the police and the neighborhood," Johnson said.

Soon even Vance agreed that the riot squad was bad business. "They're not feared, like the TMU (Tactical Mobil Unit), but they're just as hated."

Locke returned. He and Conyers talked to Police Commissioner

Ray Girardin on the phone. By 11:20 the riot squad had been moved a block south.

The group talked about what the men on the bullhorns should say. But the bullhorns were distributed before any consensus was reached.

"Meet back here at 12:30," someone shouted as the four cars pulled out. Not everyone got the message.

Conyers, followed by most of the reporters, went in one car. Witherspoon, Locke, and precinct delegate Robert Stott were in the other three.

But the loudspeakers couldn't be heard when the cars were moving, and when they stopped the speakers were jeered, stoned, or, most disheartening of all, ignored.

Conyers, beset by conflicting advice from his rather large entourage, had the roughest time.

"Tell them to meet at Trinity Church," one volunteer adviser said.

"No, tell them more police are coming," said another.

"Call a mass meeting."

"Bawl them out."

"Plead with them."

Someone boosted Conyers up to the hood of the car.

*   *   *

At Hazelwood and Twelfth there were shouts of: "We don't want to hear it."

Conyers said he'd try to get all white policemen to leave. "We're with you," he said on the mike.

"No, no, no," came the cries from the crowd.

Bottles smashed on the curb. A rock hit a nearby patrolman.

His friends helped Conyers down from the car.

Mobs Run Amuck

The following accounts relate the different kinds of activity in which mobs engage once actual rioting breaks out.

Atlanta, July 22, 1906

[From the *Atlanta Constitution*, September 24, 1906.]

It is admitted by all who saw the mob that the large majority of those in it were minors. It was Saturday night and the boys had their week's wages and a few drinks. They started in for a night of negro chasing and this was all that was done for nearly two hours.

The first disorder was at the corner of Pryor and Decatur streets, when some of the youths attacked a negro bicycle messenger. The police had to rescue the boy. From that time on the mob chased negroes along Decatur and Pryor streets and Central avenue until the fire department produced an artificial rainstorm. The mob at that time numbered about 2,000.

It was believed that the mob had dispersed and that all further danger of a serious outbreak was passed.

Then came the trolley car with negro passengers and the real danger of the night was at hand.

When the attacks were made on the street cars other men joined the mob, men who were actuated by the feeling of hatred for the race to which belonged the negro brutes who had assaulted white women. It is believed by the police that the men who boarded the trolley cars and attacked the negros had not up to that time had any connection with the mob. They were infuriated by the sight of negro men riding with white women.

From that time on the whole complexion of the mob changed and the police had an element and a situation to deal with which had not before confronted them. None realized this more than did Chief Jennings. He leaped upon the first car which the mob raided and had a hand to hand fight with the men who were trying to kill the negro men.

The mob then numbered about 3,000.

Chicago, 1919

[From *The Négro in Chicago*, p. 507.]

Few clashes occurred on Monday morning. People of both races went to work as usual and even continued to work side by side, as customary, without signs of violence. But as the afternoon wore on, white men and boys living between the Stock Yards and the "Black Belt" sought malicious amusement in directing mob violence against Negro workers returning home.

Street-car routes, especially transfer points, were thronged with white people of all ages. Trolleys were pulled from wires and the cars brought under the control of mob leaders. Negro passengers were dragged to the street, beaten, and kicked. The police were apparently powerless to cope with these numerous assaults. Four Negro men and one white assailant were killed, and thirty Negro men were severely beaten in the street-car clashes.

The "Black Belt" contributed its share of violence to the record of Monday afternoon and night. Rumors of white depredations and killings were current among the Negroes and led to acts of retaliation. An aged Italian peddler, one Lazzeroni, was set upon by young Negro boys and stabbed to death. Eugene Temple, white laundryman, was stabbed to death and robbed by three Negroes.

*   *   *

At this point, Monday night, both whites and Negroes showed signs of panic. Each race grouped by itself. Small mobs began systematically in various neighborhoods to terrorize and kill. Gangs in the white districts grew bolder, finally taking the offensive in raids through territory "invaded" by Negro home seekers. Boys between sixteen and twenty-two banded together to enjoy the excitement of the chase.

Automobile raids were added to the rioting Monday night. Cars from which rifle and revolver shots were fired were driven at great speed through sections inhabited by Negroes. Negroes defended themselves by "sniping" and volley-firing from ambush and barricade. So great was the fear of these raiding parties that the Negroes distrusted all motor vehicles and frequently opened fire on them without waiting to learn the intent of the occupants. This type of warfare was kept up spasmodically all Tuesday and was resumed with vigor Tuesday night.

At midnight, Monday, street-car clashes ended by reason of a general strike on the surface and elevated lines. The street-railway tie-up was complete for the remainder of the week. But on Tuesday morning this was a new source of terror for those who tried to walk to their places of employment. Men were killed en route to their work through hostile territory. Idle men congregated on the streets, and gang-rioting increased. A white gang of soldiers and sailors in uniform, augmented by civilians, raided the "loop," or downtown section of Chicago, early Tuesday, killing two Negroes and beating and robbing several others. In the course of these activities they wantonly destroyed property of white business men.

Gangs sprang up as far south as Sixty-third Street in Englewood and in the section west of Wentworth Avenue near Forty-seventh Street. Premeditated depredations were the order of the night. Many Negro homes in mixed districts were attacked, and several of them were burned. Furniture was stolen or destroyed. When raiders were driven off they would return again and again until their designs were accomplished.

Atlanta, July 22, 1906

[From the *Atlanta Constitution*, September 23, 1906.]

One of the worst battles of the night was that which took place around the postoffice. Here the mob, yelling for blood, rushed upon a negro barber shop just across from the federal building.

"Get 'em. Get 'em all." With this for their slogan, the crowd, armed with heavy clubs, canes, revolvers, several rifles, stones and weapons of every description, made a rush upon the negro barber shop. Those in the first line of the crowd made known their coming by throwing bricks and stones that went crashing through the windows and glass doors.

Hard upon these missiles rushed such a sea of angry men and boys as swept everything before them.

The two negro barbers working at their chairs made no effort to meet the mob. One man held up both his hands. A brick caught him in the face, and at the same time shots were fired. Both men fell to the floor. Still unsatisfied, the mob rushed into the barber shop, leaving the place a mass of ruins.

The bodies of both barbers were first kicked and then dragged from the place. Grabbing at their clothing, this was soon torn from them, many of the crowd taking these rags of shirts and clothing home as souvenirs or waving them above their heads to invite further riot.

When dragged into the street, the faces of both barbers were terribly mutilated, while the floor of the shop was wet with puddles of blood. On and on these bodies were dragged across the street to where the new building of the electric and gas company stands. In the alleyway leading by the side of this building the bodies were thrown together and left there.

At about this same time another portion of the mob busied itself with one negro caught upon the streets. He was summarily treated. Felled with a single blow, shots were fired at the body until the crowd for its own safety called for a halt on this method, and yelled, "Beat 'em up. Beat 'em up. You'll kill good white men by shooting."

By way of reply, the mob began beating the body of the negro, which was already far beyond any possibility of struggle or pain. Satisfied that the negro was dead, his body was thrown by the side of the two negro barbers and left there, the pile of three making a ghastly monument to the work of the night, and almost within the shadow of the monument of Henry W. Grady.

Just at the corner of Marietta and Forsyth streets, a negro was discovered trying to slink southward under the protection of the heavy shadows.

"There goes one!" was the cry, and the entire mob rushed from the three dead negroes at the alleyway back of the postoffice in pursuit of the black man.

Realizing that there was no possible hope of making any appeal to the mob, the negro started to run toward the Forsyth street viaduct. Instantly several bullets were fired. Evidently these went wild, as the negro kept on running, and was making some headway.

Then from the southern side of the bridge came the cries of several white men, who cried: "Stop shooting, and we'll stop him. We'll kill the black _____. He'll get away if you don't stop shooting, and let us at him."

Seeming to realize the truth of this statement, the mob on the north side of the bridge, still in pursuit, yelled: "We've done stopped shooting, stop the nigger!"

All of this in a few seconds. Then just before the negro was leaving the bridge, a man stepped from the shadow and protection of one of the iron beams of the bridge, and came down upon the negro's skull with a club, the sound of contact being heard for a block.

The black man dropped like a shot, and the mob was on him. Then the body was kicked and dragged away for a few yards, two or three members of the mob standing directly over the body, and pouring the contents of their revolvers into it.

Tulsa, May 31, 1921

[From the *Tulsa Tribune*, June 3, 1921.]

Evidence of the complete collapse of the law enforcement organization in the face of the growing riots of Tuesday night and Wednesday morning continued to pile up today.

J. P. Roberts, principal of Sequoyah school on the north side, declared today that at 9:30 Wednesday morning he called Chief of police Gustafson and told him that three or four policemen could prevent the burning and sacking of the best negro residential district—between Easton and Fairview avenues on North Detroit—if sent to the scene at once. Richards declared that the chief promised him he would send the officers immediately.

"The call was made from my office in the school," Richards said today. "I had just come from the negro quarter and I rushed back there to await the officers. They never came and very shortly a band of four or five [white] men—there were only four or five in the party —started to systematically fire the houses. They broke in the front doors and windows and presumably set fire to the bed clothing and mattresses. A few armed policemen could have easily dispersed these men.

"Systematic looting followed these fire brands. Forty or fifty men were in the looting party. They would dash into the houses and carry away everything of value they could find. Out of one house they took a piano and carted it away. I saw an automobile stolen from another home. Many trunks, valises and rugs were taken. One man came out of one of the first houses fired with a small tin box. He broke it open, took out a lot of money and small papers, threw the box and the papers away and shoved the money into his pocket and went on.

"One guardsman appeared here at 10 o'clock, after the arson and looting had been accomplished."

Detroit, July 23, 1967

[From the Kerner Report, p. 51.]

Some evidence that criminal elements were organizing spontaneously to take advantage of the riot began to manifest itself. A number of cars were noted to be returning again and again, their occupants methodically looting stores. Months later, goods stolen during the riot were still being peddled.

A spirit of carefree nihilism was taking hold. To riot and to destroy appeared more and more to become ends in themselves. Late Sunday afternoon it appeared to one observer that the young people were "dancing amidst the flames."

A Negro plainclothes officer was standing at an intersection when a man threw a Molotov cocktail into a business establishment at the corner. In the heat of the afternoon, fanned by the 20 to 25 m.p.h. winds of both Sunday and Monday, the fire reached the home next door within minutes. As residents uselessly sprayed the flames with garden hoses, the fire jumped from roof to roof of adjacent two- and three-story buildings. Within the hour the entire block was in flames. The ninth house in the burning row belonged to the arsonist who had thrown the Molotov cocktail.

In some areas residents organized rifle squads to protect firefighters. Elsewhere, especially as the wind-whipped flames began to overwhelm the Detroit Fire Department and more and more residences burned, the firemen were subjected to curses and rock-throwing.

Memphis, May, 1866

[From *Memphis Riots and Massacres*, p. 162.]

CYNTHIA TOWNSEND (colored) sworn and examined.
   By the CHAIRMAN:

2207. Where do you live? On Rayburn Avenue, Memphis.

2208. How long have you been in Memphis? About eighteen years.

2209. Have you been a slave? Yes; but I worked and bought myself. I finished paying for myself a few days before they took this place.

2210. Were you here at the time of the riot; if so, state what you saw? Yes. It was right before my door; I do not believe I could express what I saw. On Tuesday evening, the first of May, the riot began. I saw them shooting and firing. On Wednesday morning I saw man by the name of Roach, a policeman, shoot a negro man; he was driving a dray. Mr. Roach ran up and shot him right in the side of his head. I saw Mr. Cash on Wednesday morning when he shot a man by the name of Charley Wallace. Charley ran down to the bayou; came back; and as he turned the corner of my house, Mr. Cash shot him in the back part of the head. They went up to him, turned his pocket inside-out, and took out his pocket-book.

2211. Where were the policemen? I do not know the policemen only by the star they wear. I know Mr. Cash. I did not see any other men killed. When the old man Pendergrast was burning up the houses there, I saw them shoot a young girl; I could not say who did it. She fell right between two houses standing close together, and the houses were burned down right over her. I saw the Pendergrasts burning and plundering until broad daylight. The colored people were trying to get out of the houses. They told them that if they came out they would kill them. They fired into one house at a woman. She said, "Please, master, let me out." He said, "If you don't go back I'll blow your damned brains out." She went back. They set the house on fire. She just broke right out, and they all fired at her as fast as they could. I saw Mr. Pendergrast's son Pat fire at her as soon as she came in sight. This girl Rachael who was shot and burned was a nice, smart girl; I could not tell you how old she was; she was quite a young woman.

Don't Put That Fire Out

Local fire departments have not always been appreciated when they arrive at conflagrations ignited by rioters. And local policemen have been confronted with challenges that usually exceed their capacities. [From the McCone Report, pp. 19–20.]

Los Angeles, July 13–14, 1965

Friday was the worst night. The riot moved out of the Watts area and burning and looting spread over wide areas of Southeast Los

Angeles several miles apart. At 1:00 a.m. Saturday, there were 100 engine companies fighting fires in the area. Snipers shot at firemen as they fought new fires. That night, a fireman was crushed and killed on the fire line by a falling wall, and a deputy sheriff was killed when another sheriff's shotgun was discharged in a struggle with rioters.

Friday night, the law enforcement officials tried a different tactic. Police officers made sweeps on foot, moving en masse along streets to control activity and enable firemen to fight fires. By midnight, Friday, another 1,000 National Guard troops were marching shoulder to shoulder clearing the streets. By 3:00 a.m. Saturday, 3,356 guardsmen were on the streets, and the number continued to increase until the full commitment of 13,900 guardsmen was reached by midnight on Saturday. The maximum commitment of the Los Angeles Police Department during the riot period was 934 officers; the maximum for the Sheriff's Office was 719 officers.

Despite the new tactics and added personnel, the area was not under control at any time on Friday night, as major calls of looting, burning, and shooting were reported every two to three minutes. On throughout the morning hours of Saturday and during the long day, the crowds of looters and patterns of burning spread out and increased still further until it became necessary to impose a curfew on the 46.5 square-mile area on Saturday. Lieutenant Governor Anderson appeared on television early Saturday evening to explain the curfew, which made it a crime for any unauthorized persons to be on the streets in the curfew area after 8:00 p.m.

Tulsa, June 1, 1921

[From the *Tulsa Tribune,* June 1, 1921.]

At 7:30 o'clock this morning the entire south side of the negro quarter, on either side of Archer, extending from Boston east to Elgin, was a mass of flames. Firemen were helpless to combat the flames which were raging over a wide area.

"We can't use the equipment we have and for that reason have not asked for fire apparatus from other cities," Chief R. C. Alder said at 10 o'clock.

"It would mean a fireman's life to turn a stream of water on one of those negro buildings. They shot at us all morning when we were trying to do something but none of my men were hit. There is not a chance in the world to get through that mob into the negro district.

"We have five lines protecting the warehouses on the Katy railroad and I think we have them saved. If the wind should change the white residence section east of the negro district would be menaced.

"The fire has swept Greenwood street, where the negro business section was located and is sweeping around the hill to the north. So far the white residence section on the north has not been touched."

Chief Alder indicated that he was prepared to call for outside assistance in case it became necessary.

Following the fighting last night white men everywhere were heard threatening to wipe out "Little Africa" forever with the torch. The first attempt was made at 1:00 this morning when two shacks at Archer and Boston which had been used as a garrison by more than fifty blacks burst into flames.

An alarm was sent in and the department dashed to the scene. An attempt to lay hose was quickly stopped by the 500 armed white men who had assembled and the fire equipment was returned to the station while the crowd turned again to exchanging shots at long range with the blacks who were slowly retreating to the north and east behind the crowded buildings of the district.

The start to make good the threat in earnest was at 6:40 o'clock this morning. Almost simultaneously fire began to steal from the windows and doors of the deserted shacks along Archer and soon dense clouds of smoke were enveloping the entire district. Under the smoke veil armed men scouted in automobiles and on foot as their cordon tightened about the places where the blacks were stationed and occasional firing gave warning that the fight was still on.

Negroes remained in many of the burning homes until they were enveloped by the fire and threatened to fall. Then they could be seen by scores, darting from doors with their hands upraised and crying "Don't shoot," as they dashed through the smoke to surrender and be taken to the prison camp established at Convention hall. It is reported that several whites and blacks were wounded here.

Detroit, July, 1967

[From the Kerner Report, pp. 52–53.]

In the midst of chaos, there were some unexpected individual responses.

Twenty-four-year-old E.G., a Negro born in Savannah, Georgia, had come to Detroit in 1965 to attend Wayne State University. Rebellion had been building in him for a long time because,

> You just had to bow down to the white man. . . . When the insurance man would come by he would always call out to my mother by her first name and we were expected to smile and greet him happily. . . . Man, I know he would never have thought of me or my

father going to his house and calling his wife by her first name. Then I once saw a white man slapping a young pregnant Negro woman on the street with such force that she just spun around and fell. I'll never forget that.

When a friend called to tell him about the riot on 12th Street, E.G. went there expecting "a true revolt," but was disappointed as soon as he saw the looting begin: "I wanted to see the people really rise up in revolt. When I saw the first person coming out of the store with things in his arms, I really got sick to my stomach and wanted to go home. Rebellion against the white suppressors is one thing, but one measly pair of shoes or some food completely ruins the whole concept."

E.G. was standing in a crowd, watching firemen work, when Fire Chief Alvin Wall called out for help from the spectators. E.G. responded. His reasoning was: "No matter what color someone is, whether they are green or pink or blue, I'd help them if they were in trouble. That's all there is to it."

He worked with the firemen for four days, the only Negro in an all-white crew. Elsewhere, at scattered locations, a half dozen other Negro youths pitched in to help the firemen.

The Police Pitch In

New York City, July 14–15, 1863

[From George W. Walling, *Recollections of a New York Chief of Police* (Caxton Book Concern, Limited, 1887), pp. 80–82.]

That day I was directed to proceed with my men—one hundred in number—to certain buildings in the Twentieth and Twenty-second wards which were to be protected. We marched up Broadway, being supported by a company of regulars from the Invalid Corps. . . . We marched up to Forty-fifth Street, and through it to Fifth Avenue. We were confronted by a howling mob of men and women, numbering over 2000. A large number were armed with bludgeons. There was but one thing to do, and that was done quickly. I shouted out at the top of my voice, so that the rioters could hear me:

"Kill every man who has a club. Double quick. Charge!"

And at them we went with our clubs. The rioters dropped their bludgeons, tumbling over each other, and took to their heels.

We took no prisoners, but left the rioters where they fell. The number of broken heads was large. The mob dispersed in all directions, despite the frenzied cries of the women for the men to "stand up and give the police _____."

This scrimmage, however, was nothing compared with what was to follow.

Early the next day, Wednesday, at the request of General Sanford, I conveyed a large number of colored persons, who had taken refuge in the Arsenal, to my station. This was crowded already, but I managed to stow them away somehow, the officers and men giving up their rooms. Barricades had been erected by the mob on Ninth Avenue, at certain intervals, all the way from Twenty-sixth to Forty-second Street. These obstructions were constructed of carts, bricks, wagons, etc., the vehicles being lashed together with telegraph wires, or anything else that came to hand. Many of the rioters had fire-arms. They could be seen not only behind the barricades, but on the house-tops.

My instructions were simply to "clear the streets," and a company of Zouaves having been sent to support us, we proceeded to obey orders. We advanced towards the first barricade at the "double quick" with the soldiers in our rear. When within a short distance of it we were greeted by a sharp volley of pistol shots, with an occasional bullet from a musket by way of variety. Fortunately most of the balls passed over our heads, but it was warm work. The barricade could not be carried by the police alone, so we deployed to the right and left, thus allowing the soldiers space in which to manoeuvre and return the fire of the mob. This they did, and the rioters retreated.

Barricade No. 1 was won.

East St. Louis, July 2, 1917

[From *East St. Louis Riots, in Congressional Record,* Vol. 56, pt. 9, p. 8829.]

When the lawlessness began to assume serious proportions on July 2, the police instantly could have quelled and dispersed the crowds, then made up of small groups; but they either fled into the safety of a cowardly seclusion, or listlessly watched the depredations of the mob, passively and in many instances actively sharing in its work.

The testimony of every witness who was free to tell the truth agreed in condemnation of the police for failure to even halfway do their duty. They fled the scene where murder and arson held full sway. They deserted the station house and could not be found when calls for help came from every quarter of the city. The organization broke

down completely; and so great was the indifference of the few policemen who remained on duty that the conclusion is inevitable that they
shared the lust of the mob for negro blood, and encouraged the rioters
by their conduct, which was sympathetic when it was not cowardly.

*   *   *

Many other cases of police complicity in the riots could be cited.
Instead of being guardians of the peace they became a part of the
mob by countenancing the assaulting and shooting down of defenseless
negroes and adding to the terrifying scenes of rapine and slaughter.

Their disgraceful conduct was the logical fruit of the notorious alliance between the City Hall and the criminal elements, aided by
saloons, gambling houses and houses of prostitution.

Detroit, July 31, 1967

[From an Associated Press wire release by Bernard Gavzer, July 31,
1967.]

Shotgun resting on his hip, the white, bareheaded, burly Detroit
policeman brusquely told a fidgeting, perspiring Negro to beat it
and the man backed away, saying, "Yes, sir. Yes, sir."

The policeman found it refreshing.

"It's been the first time in 10 years them niggers are saying 'Yes,
sir. No, sir.' They are 'sirring' us up, down, sideways and backward."

His candid hostility against Negroes was not, and is not, unique
among some of Detroit's white police. To this reporter, dozens of
officers expressed the same contempt for Negroes.

*   *   *

There is a sort of white Public Enemy No. 1 for the white police:
"Jerry, . . ." They say with considerable disgust. Mayor Jerome
Cavanagh.

"We could have put this thing down without National Guard and
without state troopers and without a single one of those fancy combat
veterans, but City Hall—our man, Jerry—it's like telling us, 'Oh, no,
do not touch them, don't say a mean word, you'll hurt their feelings."

Could the police have prevented any widespread outbreak? Could
they have done the job using any new equipment or techniques that
wouldn't have produced a toll of 39 dead?

"You must be an idiot," one cop said. "We've got plenty, but that doesn't mean we're ever going to use any of it until the politicians wake up.

"Hell, I'm standing on the street Sunday and watching people looting, and I'm under orders not to fire. You think I'm going to go in there against that mob with my stock? No, I just stand there and watch them carry away anything they want and as far as I'm concerned that no-fire order is the same as telling me that when I see a looter, I'm supposed to say, 'Oh, Mr. Looter, is that too heavy for you? Be careful you do not trip taking that color TV out of the man's store.'"

He said the police had tear gas that could be used, but wasn't. Fire hoses could have been used to break up gangs of looters, he said, but they weren't. The one thing that police have that could have stopped it from the very beginning, he said, was the shotgun and rifle. Teargas was subsequently used, not against any groups of people, but to try to flush a sniper from an apartment house.

"If Whitey was calling the shots," said one Negro, "You'd have 15 times as many people dead. That's what he likes to do, to kill the brother."

Both black and white police said they were ready to quit the force, or wanted to. They said there were many others who felt the same way. Could that be true of all the 4,200 men in the department? No one had a number, but they said the feeling was widespread.

And intense: during the brief flurry of sniping early in the fifth morning a group of National Guardsmen and police were pinned down near 12th Street and Taylor. There was a lull and in the bleak silence of the darkness, some piece of rubble in the charred carcass of a building gave way. A helmeted policeman saw some guardsmen swing as though they were expecting an attack and without turning his head told them to take it easy. Then, with disgust, he said:

"Let them have this nigger town."

Detroit, June 20–21, 1943

[From Thurgood Marshall, "The Gestapo in Detroit," *The Crisis* (August, 1943), pp. 232–33.]

THE RIOT SPREADS TO DETROIT PROPER

A short time after midnight disorder broke out in a white neighborhood near the Roxy Theatre on Woodward Avenue. The Roxy is an all night theatre attended by white and Negro patrons. Several Ne-

groes were beaten and others were forced to remain in the theatre for
lack of police protection. The rumor spread among the white people
that a Negro had raped a white woman on Belle Island and that the
Negroes were rioting.

At about the same time a rumor spread around Hastings and Adams
Streets in the Negro area that white sailors had thrown a Negro
woman and her baby into the lake at Belle Isle and that the police
were beating Negroes. This rumor was also repeated by an unidentified
Negro at one of the Negro night spots. Some Negroes began to attack
white persons in the area. The police immediately began to use their
sticks and revolvers against these Negroes. The Negroes began to
break out the windows of stores of white merchants on Hastings
Street.

The interesting thing is that when the windows in the stores on
Hastings Street were first broken, there was no looting. An officer of
the Merchants' Association walked the length of Hastings Street starting out at 7 o'clock Monday morning and noticed that none of the
stores with broken windows had been looted. It is thus clear that the
original breaking of windows was not for the purpose of looting.
Throughout Monday the Detroit police, instead of placing policemen
in front of the stores to protect them from looting, contented themselves with driving up and down Hastings Street from time to time
and stopping in front of the stores. The usual procedure was to jump
out of the squad cars with drawn revolvers and riot guns to shoot
whoever might be in the store. The policemen would then tell the
Negro bystanders to "run and not look back." On several occasions,
persons running were shot in the back. In other instances, bystanders
were clubbed by police. To the Detroit police, all Negroes on Hastings
Street were "looters." This included war workers returning from work.
There is no question that some Negroes were guilty of looting just
as there is always looting during earthquakes or as looting occurred
when English towns were bombed by the Germans.

Woodward Avenue is one of the main thoroughfares of the city of
Detroit. Small groups of white people began to rove up and down
Woodward Avenue beating Negroes, stoning cars containing Negroes,
stopping streets [sic] cars and yanking Negroes from them, and stab-
bing and shooting Negroes. In no case did the police do more than
try to "reason" with these mobs, many of which were at this stage
quite small. The police did not draw their revolvers or riot guns, and
never used any force to disperse these mobs. As a result of this, the
mobs got larger and bolder and even attacked Negroes on the pave-
men [sic] of the City Hall in demonstration not only of their contempt for law and order as represented by the municipal govern-

ment. The use of night sticks or the drawing of revolvers would have dispersed these white groups and saved the lives of many Negroes. It would not have been necessary to shoot, but it would have been sufficient to threaten to shoot into the white mobs. The use of a fire hose would have dispersed many of the groups. None of these things were done and the disorder took on the proportions of a major riot. The responsibility of this rests with the Detroit police.

At the height of the disorder on Woodward Avenue, Negroes driving north on Brush Street (a Negro street) were stopped at Vernor Highway by a policeman who forced them to detour to Woodward Avenue. Many of these cars are automobiles which appeared in the pictures released by several newspapers showing them overturned and burned on Woodward Avenue.

*   *   *

One Negro, who has been an employee of a bank in Detroit for the past eighteen years, was on his way to work on a Woodward Avenue street car when he was seized by one of the white mobs. In the presence of at least four policemen, he was beaten and stabbed in the side. He also heard several shots fired from the back of the mob. He managed to run to two of the policemen, who proceeded to "protect" him from the mob. The two policemen, followed by two mounted policemen, proceeded down Woodward Avenue. While he was being escorted by these policemen, the Negro was struck in the face by at least eight of the mob, and at no time was any effort made to prevent him from being struck. After a short distance this man noticed a squad car parked on the other side of the street. In sheer desperation, he broke away from the two policemen who claimed to be protecting him and ran to the squad car begging for protection. The officer in the squad car put him in the back seat and drove off, thereby saving this man's life. During all this time, the fact that the man was either shot or stabbed was evident because of the fact that blood was spurting from his side. Despite this obvious felony, committed in the presence of at least four policemen, no effort was made at that time either to protect the victim or since to arrest the persons guilty of the felony.

Call the National Guard

National Guard troops, arriving later while a riot is in full swing, can help or hinder.

Chicago, July 28–August 8, 1919

[From *The Negro in Chicago*, pp. 41–42.]

The militia had been given special drills in the suppression of riots and insurrections for a year and a half previous to this occasion, and were, in the estimation of their commanding officer, "Probably better prepared for riot drill than any troops ever put on duty in the state."

The activities of the militia did not begin as early as many citizens wished. Though troops began to mobilize in the armories on Monday night, July 28, they were not called to actual duty on the streets until 10:30 P.M., Wednesday, July 20. When called to active duty they were distributed in the areas of conflict. Between 5,000 and 6,000 troops were called out. This number was made up entirely of white troops. . . . Colored troops who had composed the Eighth Regiment were not reorganized at that time, and therefore none participated.

*   *   *

The manner in which the militia was received by various elements in the communities where stationed is illuminating. Police officers were glad that the troops came to relieve them. Two policemen on duty with a patrol exclaimed, when they heard the militia had come in force, "Thank God! We can't stand up under this much longer!" The police at Cottage Grove Avenue said, "We are tickled to death to see you fellows come in; you have never looked so good to us before!" A regimental commander said his organization was "welcomed into the zone, of course, by everybody, and I'd say especially by the colored people." A similar report came from another regimental commander.

But there was some show of hostility to the troops. Hoodlums fired on some detachments when they first came in, and Colonel Bolte reported a hatred for the troops by "the Hamburg Athletic Club, the Ragen's, and the Emeralds, and a whole bunch of them over there who didn't like to be controlled. . . ."

The militia unquestionably prevented mob formations, raids, and "sniping." They checked marauders still in search of prey. In many cases they prevented the initial moves of lawlessness by taking stations at critical points long before raiders arrived.

There was a marked contrast between the militia and the police. The troops were under definite orders; commanders had absolute control of their forces and knew at all times where and how many effectives were available at hand. Discipline was always good. Only one person, a white man, was killed by the troops. Whatever other restraining causes contributed, it is certain that the riot was not revived after the troops were posted.

Most of the troops were withdrawn on August 8.

Detroit, July 27, 1967

[From the *Detroit Free Press*, July 28, 1967.]

"All right, let's move out," Tack said. A jeep with mounted machine gun took the point. Behind the captain, a truck carried Guardsmen to walk posts on the darkest, most menacing streets. A noisy M41 tank brought up the rear.

The air was balmy, with a hint of coming rain and the odor of burnt-out buildings. The tank, the bristling muzzles of guns at the ready, and the dark old buildings along Twelfth were silhouetted against the sky.

"It's like in the movies," said the clean-cheeked Guardsman riding behind the driver. He was nervous, excited, and he said aloud that his buddies were "hoping for some action."

On Fourteenth, at LaSalle Gardens, police officers and other Guardsmen were crouched behind their vehicles. The jeep pulled over. Everybody piled out and crouched because everyone else was crouching.

"What's up?" Tack called.

"Supposed to be a sniper. That big red brick house on the corner."

It was dark and silent, except when someone took off, running for better position.

On the porch of a battered house, a Negro couple and their covey of kids watched the scene. It was better than television.

A policeman, armed with a shotgun, came by, running low.

"Get back in that house," he yelled. "Watcha trying to do? Get yourselves killed?"

He didn't understand that they had no fear of snipers. They disappeared into the dark house, in fear of the police.

No one could say for sure that a shot had come from the brick house. Tack got tired of crouching against nothing, so he left.

Sgt. John Mielke, his driver, headed back to Hutchins. Suddenly some tracers cut through the night sky like fireworks. Mielke headed for the curb and jumped it, bouncing Tack violently.

"Damn it," he said, with a little humor, "nobody's firing at us. Now come on, nerves, let's get back to headquarters."

At the school, as another patrol was setting out, an officer ordered his machine gunner to lock and load. The gunner racked the bolt back and Guardsmen dived for cover as the .30 caliber slugs splattered the walls of the school.

Elsewhere in the yard Guardsmen were taking pot shots at an outside light which they feared illuminated them for snipers.

Someone suggested that instead of shooting they find the switch and turn it off. When they couldn't find it, nor the custodian who mourned for his building, Tack dispatched the bulb with a shot from his M1.

Throughout the long night no one was ever certain whether the shots they heard came from the police, Guardsmen or snipers.

Out on patrol again, there was a call at Twelfth and Taylor: "A sniper has an Army bus pinned down."

Fifty Guardsmen and police took cover around the suspected building—a two-story walkup with a store below. As a Guardsman jumped from a jeep, he flicked the safety catch on his rifle and accidentally pulled the trigger. Everybody ducked.

"What's going on?" Tack yelled.

"I don't know," came the answer from the dark. "Sniper, I guess."

Tack took Mielke around the back of the building, hollering a warning to keep from being shot at by his other men.

The tank rumbled up, turned ominously to face the building, and opened up with its .50 caliber. The tracers sliced into the building from top to bottom, smashing a light standard in front.

The tank topped the tottering standard as a safety precaution, then drew back while police and Guardsmen entered the building.

There was a single shot from a small-caliber weapon.

"That's the sniper. The bastard's still there," someone whispered.

"Naw," came an answer. "I heard the sniper was using an automatic weapon."

"Did you hear it? Did he hit the bus?"

"I don't know. Somebody else said they heard the shots."

Tack, sweating, came back with police.

"Nobody in there," said the captain.

"I guess they're firing one shot and running," said a disgusted officer.

The fuzzy-cheeked soldier, thereafter, didn't jump from the jeep every time it stopped. He was beginning to feel silly. And Mielke, who had to stay with his captain, kept forgetting to take his rifle.

There was a traffic accident at Third and Grand. Things seemed to be quieting, returning to normal. An Army truck had hit a white Thunderbird, and the drivers were standing under the street lights exchanging license numbers.

There was a shot from somewhere. As Tack's jeep pulled up short alongside a van from WWJ News, soldiers, police and the driver of the Thunderbird were crouched behind the truck and battered car.

Three police officers opened up on the street light above them, and the newsman from WWJ was telling his office on the radio telephone: "We're at Third and the Boulevard, and we're under fire, pinned down."

Tack heard it and laughed, and ordered his jeep to go elsewhere.

"It's real quiet tonight," he said. And like the proprietor of a fishing camp, he added: "You should have been here this afternoon."

Tulsa, June 1, 1921

[Frank Van Voorhis, Capt., to L. J. F. Rooney, Lt. Col. 3rd Inf. Okla. Natl. Gd., "Detailed Report of Negro Uprising for Service Company, 3d Inf. Okla. Natl. Gd.," July 30, 1921.]

. . . After ordering the men not to fire until ordered to do so, I proceeded East on Cameron Street with a civilian driver in a touring car; had not gone far when I was convinced that the troops under Capt. McCuen and Lt. Wood had not gone that route, so I continued on to Greenwood Avenue, turned North on Greenwood Avenue, and proceeded North three (3) blocks when I discovered negroes fleeing to the Northeast. We immediately proceeded to overtake them and when overtaken they were commanded to halt and put up their hands, which orders were promptly complied with. I detailed two (2) men to disarm and guard them until further orders. A few blocks further North I discovered more armed negroes, and having overtaken and disarmed them, sent my men in various directions with orders to search all houses for negroes and fire arms. Had between twenty (20) and thirty (30) negro prisoners under guard when the white civilians on Sun Set Hill opened fire on us and caused us to suspend operations at that point. Ordered men with the prisoners to double time South about one-fourth block and halted them behind a new concrete building for protection. Firing shortly ceased somewhat and we double timed further South on Greenwood Avenue, out of range and waited until police patrol cars arrived. I turned prisoners over to the deputies, about thirty-five or forty (40) in number, with orders to take them to Police headquarters. Then with my six (6) men marched North on Greenwood Avenue three (3) blocks. We then proceeded up Sun Set Hill, and when about two-thirds (⅔) of the way up the hill, the negroes to the North opened fire on us, slightly wounding Sgt. Len Stone and Sgt. Ed. Sanders. We continued our march without returning their fire and upon arriving at the crest of the hill found Service and Co. B, deployed there in a prone position with old machine gun in position. I then called for volunteers to accompany me down the hill into the negro settlement; then with twelve (12) selected men I started down the hill when my attention was drawn to the white civilians to the northeast of me who had opened fire again on the negro settlement. Halting my men, I returned to where Capt. McCuen and 1st Lt. Wood were and ordered Capt. McCuen to see that the civilians immediately ceased firing. After the firing ceased, with my detail, I went down into the negro settlement, about 8:00 o'clock A.M. deployed my men along Davenport Street, with orders to search every house to the right and left for negroes and fire arms. About two (2) blocks from there we established a post (receiving station for prisoners) this was located at the intersection of Greenwood Avenue and Davenport Streets, and after taking thirty (30) or forty (40) prisoners, they were placed under guard and marched to Police headquarters by a detail of my men. I then proceeded with a portion of my detachment North on Greenwood Avenue, taking prisoners all along the street.

Among the first prisoners captured by my men was a negro doctor named Chas. B. Wickham, who proved to be a very valuable aid in having the negroes surrender to me, which they willingly did upon finding out we were there to protect them and to preserve order and after getting together about one hundred fifty (150) negro prisoners, I detailed St. James N. Concannon, with four (4) men to proceed North to the negro park as I had been informed a number of negroes had gathered there, with orders to take all prisoners, disarm and bring them to Convention Hall where prisoners were being held at that time. Sgt. James N. Concannon accounted for one hundred seventy-one (171) prisoners, all of whom were turned over to the civil authorities. Then with seven of my men I proceeded with negro prisoners to the number of one hundred and fifty (150) to the Convention Hall by going south to the foot of Sun Set Hill, west to Main Street, South to Boulder to Convention Hall, to avoid having to pass thru a large number of civilian rioters. After turning over the prisoners to civil authorities at Convention Hall, returned with my men to the negro district, where I took more prisoners and when I got them to Convention Hall was told that the Convention Hall was full and that I would have to take them on to McNulty Park, which I did. There turned them over to the civil authorities and at about 11:00 o'clock A.M. again returned to the negro district.

*   *   *

I carried fifty (50) rounds of pistol ammunition with me at all times during the Negro Uprising but did not fire a single shot.

Newark, July 15–16, 1967

[From the Kerner Report, pp. 37–38.]

On Saturday, July 15, Spina received a report of snipers in a housing project. When he arrived he saw approximately 100 National Guardsmen and police officers crouching behind vehicles, hiding in corners and lying on the ground around the edge of the courtyard.

Since everything appeared quiet and it was broad daylight, Spina walked directly down the middle of the street. Nothing happened. As he came to the last building of the complex, he heard a shot. All around him the troopers jumped, believing themselves to be under sniper fire. A moment later a young Guardsman ran from behind a building.

The director of police went over and asked him if he had fired the shot. The soldier said yes, he had fired to scare a man away from a window; that his orders were to keep everyone away from windows.

Spina said he told the soldier: "Do you know what you just did? You have now created a state of hysteria. Every Guardsman up and down this street and every State Policeman and every city policeman that is present thinks that somebody just fired a shot and that it is probably a sniper."

A short time later more "gunshots" were heard. Investigating, Spina came upon a Puerto Rican sitting on a wall. In reply to a question as to whether he knew "where the firing is coming from?" the man said:

"That's no firing. That's fireworks. If you look up to the fourth floor, you will see the people who are throwing down these cherry bombs."

By this time four truckloads of National Guardsmen had arrrived and troopers and policemen were again crouched everywhere, looking for a sniper. The director of police remained at the scene for three hours, and the only shot fired was the one by the Guardsman.

Nevertheless, at six o'clock that evening two columns of National Guardsmen and state troopers were directing mass fire at the Hayes Housing Project in response to what they believed were snipers.

On the 10th floor, Eloise Spellman, the mother of several children, fell, a bullet through her neck.

Across the street a number of persons, standing in an apartment window, were watching the firing directed at the housing project. Suddenly several troopers whirled and began firing in the general direction of the spectators. Mrs. Hattie Gainer, a grandmother, sank to the floor.

A block away Rebecca Brown's 2-year-old daughter was standing at the window. Mrs. Brown rushed to drag her to safety. As Mrs. Brown was, momentarily, framed in the window, a bullet spun into her back.

All three women died.

A number of eye witnesses, at varying times and places, reported seeing bottles thrown from upper story windows. As these would land at the feet of an officer he would turn and fire. Thereupon, other officers and Guardsmen up and down the street would join in.

In order to protect his property, B. W. W., the owner of a Chinese laundry, had placed a sign saying "Soul Brother" in his window. Between 1:00 and 1:30 A.M., on Sunday, July 16, he, his mother, wife, and brother, were watching television in the back room. The neighborhood had been quiet. Suddenly, B. W. W. heard the sound of jeeps, then shots.

Going to an upstairs window he was able to look out in the street. There he observed several jeeps, from which soldiers and state troopers were firing into stores that had "Soul Brother" signs in the windows. During the course of three nights, according to dozens of eye witness reports, law enforcement officers shot into and smashed windows of businesses that contained signs indicating they were Negro owned.

❋   ❋   ❋

By Monday afternoon, July 17, state police and National Guard forces were withdrawn. That evening, a Catholic priest saw two Negro men walking down the street. They were carrying a case of soda and two bags of groceries. An unmarked car with five police officers pulled up beside them. Two white officers got out of the car. Accusing the Negro men of looting, the officers made them put the groceries on the sidewalk, then kicked the bags open, scattering their contents all over the street.

Telling the men, "Get out of here," the officers drove off. The Catholic priest went across the street to help gather up the groceries. One of the men turned to him: "I've just been back from Vietnam 2 days," he said, "and this is what I get. I feel like going home and getting a rifle and shooting the cops."

Of the 250 fire alarms, many had been false, and 13 were considered by the city to have been "serious." Of the $10,251,000 damage total, four-fifths was due to stock loss. Damage to buildings and fixtures was less than $2 million.

Twenty-three persons were killed—a white detective, a white fireman, and 21 Negroes. One was 73-year-old Isaac Harrison. Six were women. Two were children.

The Participants

The following selections recount the proceedings from the view-points of some of the people involved: victims, rioters, and those who preferred to avoid direct participation. [From *Memphis Riots and Massacres,* p. 161.]

Memphis, May 1, 1866

Lucy Tibbs (colored) sworn and examined.

2176. I understand you to say, then, you saw four men killed under the circumstances stated, and that you know in addition of two others being killed, and that then you saw the dead body of this girl Rachael? Yes, sir; and my brother got killed on Tuesday afternoon; who killed him I do not know.

2177. What was his name? His name was Bob Taylor. He had been a member of the 59th regiment, but was out of the service. On Tuesday afternoon when they were firing and going from house to house, I told him to try and get away if he could. He started to run away, but was found dead the next morning by that bayou just back of my house. He was older than I am. They robbed me that night of $300 of his money.

2178. Did they come into your house? Yes; a crowd of men came in that night; I do not know who they were. They just broke the door open and asked me where was my husband; I replied he was gone; they said I was a liar; I said, "Please do not do anything to me; I am just here with two little children."

2179. Did they do anything to you? They done a very bad act.

2180. Did they ravish you? Yes, sir.

2181. How many of them? There was but one that did it. Another man said, "Let that woman alone—that she was not in any situation to be doing that." They went to my trunk, burst it open, and took this money that belonged to my brother.

2182. Did they violate your person against your consent? Yes, sir; I had just to give up to them. They said they would kill me if I did not. They put me on the bed, and the other men were plundering the house while this man was carrying on.

2183. Were any of them policemen? I do not know; I was so scared I could not tell whether they were policemen or not; I think there were folks that knew all about me, who knew that my brother had not been long out of the army and had money.

2184. Where were your children? In bed.

2185. Were you dressed or undressed when these men came to you? I was dressed.

2186. Did you make any resistance? No, sir; the house was full of men. I thought they would kill me; they had stabbed a woman near by the night before.

2187. How old are your children? One of them will soon be five, and the other will be two years old in August.

2188. What did they mean by saying you was not in a condition to be doing that? I have been in the family way ever since Christmas.

Detroit, July 23, 1967

[From the Kerner Report, p. 53.]

An hour before midnight a 45-year-old white man, Walter Grzanka, together with three white companions, went into the street. Shortly thereafter a market was broken into. Inside the show window a Negro man began filling bags with groceries and handing them to confederates outside the store. Grzanka twice went over to the store, accepted bags, and placed them down beside his companions across the street. On the third occasion he entered the market. When he emerged, the market owner, driving by in his car, shot and killed him.

In Grzanka's pockets police found seven cigars, four packages of pipe tobacco, and nine pairs of shoelaces.

Chicago, July 28–31, 1919

[From *The Negro in Chicago,* pp. 656, 658, 659.]

Mob of 300 or 400 white people, all ages, attacked east-bound Forty-seventh Street car, pulled the trolley from the wire, stopped the car. White passengers alighted, Negro passengers hid under seats. From twenty-five to fifty white men boarded car and beat the Negroes with bats, clubs, bricks. Driven out from the refuge of the car, they ran for their lives, chased by the mob. Mills ran from Forty-seventh Street into Normal Avenue. A brick hit him in the back, halted him, and before he could run again a young white man hit him on the head with a scantling. He was left unconscious. Four other Negroes from this car were beaten but not fatally.

*   *   *

Scott, Brown, and Simpson, Negroes, were returning by street car from work in the Stock Yards when the car was boarded by a mob of white men who attacked the Negroes with clubs and bricks. Scott defended himself with a pocketknife, while Kleinmark tried to beat him with a club. One of the blows with the knife went home, and Kleinmark staggered from the car mortally wounded. Scott was jailed and charged with murder. The coroner's jury commented as follows: "It is the sense of this jury that the conduct of the police at the time of the riot at this point, during the subsequent investigation, and at the preliminary hearing at which Joseph Scott was bound over to the grand jury without counsel, was a travesty on justice and fair play."

*   *   *

Lovings, returning home from work on a bicycle, rode through an Italian neighborhood whose residents were much excited because it had been said earlier in the evening that a Negro employee of a mattress factory near-by had shot a little Italian girl. A mob filled the streets when Lovings was sighted. He tried to escape by running down an alley between Taylor and Gilpin streets, and then jumped back fences and hid in a basement. The mob dragged him out, riddled his body with bullets, stabbed him, and beat him. It was afterward rumored that his body had been burned after being saturated with gasoline. This was proved not to be true.

*   *   *

A mob of about 500 Negroes at Thirty-fifth Street and Wabash Avenue, was stopping cars, beating white people, and throwing bricks. An automobile bearing Otterson as a passenger turned from Thirty-fifth Street to go south on Wabash Avenue. One of the stones and bricks hurled at the motor car hit Otterson on the head, and he immediately became unconscious. He was seventy-four years old and a plasterer by trade.

East St. Louis, July 2, 1917

[From *East St. Louis Riots*, in *Congressional Record*, Vol. 56, pt. 9, p. 8828.]

At Collinsville and Illinois Avenues a negro man and his wife and 14-year-old boy were assaulted. The man was beaten to death; his head was crushed in as if by a blow from a stone, and the boy was shot and killed. The woman was very badly injured; her hair was torn out by the roots and her scalp was partly torn off by some one who took hold of the ragged edges of a wound and scalped her. After a time an ambulance drove up and the bodies of these three negroes were loaded into it. The father and the son were dead, and when the woman regained consciousness she found herself lying on the dead bodies of her husband and child. This family lived across the Mississippi River in St. Louis and were on their way home after having been on a fishing trip north of East St. Louis. They were innocent of any connection with the race feeling that brought about the riot and were victims of the savage brutality of the mob, who spared neither age nor sex in their blind lust for blood.

Detroit, July 23, 1967

[From the Kerner Report, p. 53.]

At midnight Sharon George, a 23-year-old white woman, together with her two brothers, was a passenger in a car being driven by her husband. After having dropped off two Negro friends, they were returning home on one of Detroit's main avenues when they were slowed by a milling throng in the street. A shot fired from close range struck the car. The bullet splintered in Mrs. George's body. She died less than two hours later.

Tulsa, June 1, 1921

[From the *Tulsa Tribune*, July 15, 1921.]

O. W. Gurley, negro, who said he lost $175,000 worth of business and residence property in the fire declared he looked from the window of the Gurley hotel early on the morning of June 1 and saw four white men in khaki clothes cross the Katy tracks and set fire to a number of the biggest buildings on Greenwood avenue, his three story brick hotel included.

"My wife fell," said Gurley, "as I held her by the hand. She told me to run. I thought she was killed. I ran three blocks to the Dunbar school and hid in a hole in the basement. I saw more than a thousand white men go by in a crowd. Pretty soon a man came and poked in the hole with a gun. He fired once and then said, 'he must have crawled out on the other side.' I stayed in there until they set fire to the building and the roof fell in. Then I thought it was death to stay and death to go—but finally crawled out and was taken to the ball park by a white gentleman."

Gurley told how he was taken in the armory that evening to have

his hand dressed, which he had cut on a piece of glass, and was over-
joyed to find his wife there alive and well.

"When you started for the Dunbar school did you see any one else
around?" asked Attorney Leahy.

"I just saw one man, sir," answered Gurley, "and I saw him because
he was running faster than I was and passed me. I think he is the
only man who passed me." The laughter of the crowd was suddenly
stilled when Gurley said the man was shot down just after he passed
him.

Detroit, July, 1967

[From the *Detroit Free Press*, July 28, 1967.]

"I'm wiped out," said Samuel Lipson, owner of a clothing and variety
store that stood at 8541 Twelfth.

"I'm 63. At this age, I lost everything. I don't know what I'm going
to do," he said.

Lipson's business lay in the block between Pingree and Philadelphia,
a typical block in the riot area.

Saturday night it held a fruit market, a drugstore, a hardware store,
a fish market, a drygoods store, a butcher shop, a party store selling
beer and snacks, a currency exchange, a pawnshop, a barbershop, a
record store and a cafe.

Sunday afternoon there was nothing left but the Cream of Michigan
Cafe on the corner. It's still locked and darkened.

The rest is a blackened shell and a vast pit of twisted wreckage,
smoldering fires, and foul, stagnant water seeping higher up the basement walls.

Lipson and his wife, Minnie, brought their business to Twelfth St.
five years ago, when the Chrysler Freeway robbed them of their
customers of 17 years in the old neighborhood.

He said he lost $20,000 worth of merchandise, women's clothes and
men's underwear, 49-cent-a-pair nylon stockings and $2.98 back-to-
school dresses.

His insurance expired five weeks ago. The company refused to re-
new, claiming the risk of rioting during this long, hot summer was too
great.

"We didn't expect any trouble," said Lipson. "As a matter of fact,
I was consulted by different civic groups about whether we felt there
was any trouble. In our opinion there wasn't a sign of it."

Like other businessmen on the block, Lipson bitterly blames city
officials for not ordering police to fire on the looters who sacked and
later destroyed his store.

"Cavanagh, he couldn't run for street cleaner right now as far as the businessmen are concerned," said Lipson. "The whole thing was mismanaged."

This was meant to be a week of vacation in South Haven for the Lipsons. But Monday they will have no business to go back to.

Los Angeles, July, 1965

[From the *Pittsburgh Courier*, August 28, 1965.]

The opinion of so many here was expressed by a young man who admitted starting one of the fires.

"The riots will continue because I, as a Negro, am immediately considered a criminal by police, and if I have a pretty woman with me, she's a tramp—even if she's my wife or mother," he stated bitterly. "That's the Watts Negro's status with the Los Angeles police department."

*   *   *

Along with Parker, the whole police force is being lashed by riot-battered residents. An unemployed man who admitted he had spent at least two nights throwing rocks at policemen, said, "Maybe the people of Beverly Hills would riot too if they spent most of their life with a cop's club in their face. Or if they had to get out of an automobile with their hands over their head to be questioned for doing nothing at all."

Detroit, June 21, 1943

[From the *Detroit News*, July 30, 1943. Selections from the *Detroit News* are reprinted by permission of the publisher.]

Four white youths, all but one teen-aged, were held today in the race riot murder of Moses Kiska, 58-year-old Negro shot down the evening of June 21 as he waited for a street car at Mack avenue and Chene street.

Prosecutor Dowling said he had confessions from three of the quartet. They shot Kiska, he stated, for no other reason than that they had a rifle and wanted to "have some fun shooting niggers."

Homicide squad detectives said the youths showed no more compunction about shooting Kiska than "normal men would show at going out to shoot clay pigeons."

*   *   *

"The story as I have it from the confessions is a story of cold-blooded murder," Dowling said. Trani and Mastantuano were out driving and stopped at one of their favorite hangouts, a pool room at Superior and Moran.

"They saw the two other youths, whom they said they knew as 'Bob' and 'Blackie.' The four of them got in the car.

"Mastantuano had the rifle. At Mack and Chene they saw Kiska waiting in the street car zone. Trani said to his companion, 'Give me the gun.' He leaned out of the car and fired. They saw Kiska grab his chest and topple over. They drove away, and then separated."

Detroit, July 1, 1943

[From "Bitterness of Citizens Concerning Race Riots Expressed by Alleman," by Gene Alleman, in *The Wayne Dispatch*, July 2, 1943. Reprinted by permission of the publisher.]

Cab drivers are proverbial sources of much information and gossip, and this driver—a husky white chap of about 45 years—was no exception. I started off with reference to my friend's remark about "hoodlums" who had taken over control of the city before federal troops arrived at 11 p.m. the night before.

"I'd like to have that guy say 'hoodlums' to me" he retorted quickly, turning about to give me a belligerent once-over as the cab left the curb. "Don't believe that, brother. I was in that mob last night, and I killed one of those niggers myself! I've got the iron bar right with me, too. A lot of good American citizens were in there fighting, mister."

I will not quote all the things this cab driver told me, but he did blame recent mayors of Detroit for "catering" to Negro voters and for permitting them to "over-run" Belle Isle.

"This thing will never be solved until all the niggers have been put under," he declared vehemently. "I'm going to try and get a gun, and the first nigger that comes toward my cab is going to get it, full-blast." Those were his exact words.

Washington, July 22, 1919

[From E.G.M. to *The Nation*, August 9, 1919, p. 173.]

TO THE EDITOR OF THE NATION:
   SIR:
On Tuesday night, when so many in Ledriot Park feared a mob and

a general massacre, and when most white men believed that a white woman who ventured into that section would be literally devoured, I took it into my head to go there, and go I did. I went for several reasons. One was to prove that a white woman could do it; another, because I knew what had been done by the authorities and thought that a little reassurance from a lone and harmless woman might go a good way, for I guessed the probable psychological state in that section. Besides, I wanted to know at first hand what the Negroes were doing and thinking. I found out. If I talked to one colored man, I talked to a hundred and fifty. . . .

I saw no women at all. And the men—why, those men were not out to "start something." They were armed, most of them, and were quite frank about it, but they did not want a fight. They said they were out to see if a mob were coming, and, if there were, they were going home to barricade themselves; then, if the mob tried to get in, there was trouble ahead. As one put it: "A man would be less than a man if he didn't fight for his family and his home." Their state of mind was not primarily fight. It was fear, a perfect hysteria of dread lest, as more than one expressed it, "a new East St. Louis" was at hand. And, as with all hysteria, a small occurrence would have set them off in a frenzy. Dynamite! They were TNT. Again and again I was asked: "Is a mob gathering on Pennsylvania Avenue? Will they come up and burn us out? Is the Park cordoned?" For they did not dare go downtown far enough to see if the troops were really there. Over and over, I heard the pathetic question: "Do the white folks care? Does anyone care? Are they really doing anything?" I told them that the best of the whites did care, but that we were helpless. I told them also that measures had really been taken that afternoon and what they were—that there really was military, as well as police, protection. One queer old man remarked: "Well, I reckon somebuddy do care, or a white lady wouldn't come out to tell us about it." A one-handed soldier said: "I enlisted; I gave the country my hand, and I was ready to give more. When I was in France, I was a man and a soldier, but when I get back here, I'm not a citizen; I'm not a man, even—just a big, black brute." It was not said bitterly; it went deeper than bitterness. He spoke like a man with a broken heart. Another said: "They say this is to protect the white women. My father was in charge of a whole plantation and a family of white women during the Civil War. They weren't afraid to leave the white women with us then, and Negroes are no different now."

＊   ＊   ＊

I saw but one noisy Negro, a half-witted and dishevelled-looking fellow, talking loudly and belligerently. Him two colored men seized and thoroughly shook, telling him that if he did not "shut up and get home," he would certainly find things happening to him. Once an excited Negro boy came flying on a bicycle with the news that a white mob had formed inside the cordon and was on its way. "Let's go meet them," said one young hothead. This was at once negatived. "We'll watch and see if they are coming, and if they are, we will go home and lock the doors. That's what Captain Doyle said, and he knows what's what." So, for a few tense moments, we stood peering into the drizzly gloom, not knowing what might after all be about to come. But all was quiet, and we silently drifted on our ways.

And thus it went for two hours. I met them—not savages, not red-handed murderers, but citizens, hunted and terrified, looking more or less hopelessly to their Government for aid; human beings craving the hand of brotherhood, and cut to the very heart. . . .

Memphis, May 2, 1866

[From *Memphis Riots and Massacres,* p. 72.]

407. Did you see any other negroes hurt? I was standing near the store and saw several men cross the bridge over the bayou, and meet a negro in that vicinity; they commenced beating him; he ran into a store; he said he had done nothing; they continued beating him until he managed to get out of the back door, when he ran away. Just as they came out they met another negro; he had, I think, a pan in his hand. I understood he was going to the store for meal for his family.

408. How many times did they strike him? About fifteen or twenty times, I think; any one of the blows would have killed me. They knocked him down in the gutter, when some one shot him twice, or the shots may have been fired by two different parties.

409. Who were these parties? They were white men; I could not say whether they were policemen or not, I was somewhat excited. There were a dozen men near when the beating commenced, and several others afterwards gathered around.

410. What did they do after they had shot the negro? Some of them stood around after the beating, and some walked off.

411. Did you hear any conversation? Nothing more than I heard the negro say he had done nothing.

412. With what did they strike him? Clubs, or something in their hands. It was too dark for me to be able to tell whether they wore stars or not.

413. Did you go to the place where the negro was lying? No, sir.

414. Who took him away? I do not know.

415. How long did he lay there? I was told it was done shortly after I left my store, which was between seven and eight o'clock.

416. When you went away, were there any persons about the body? I believe there were some men there.

417. Did you go near the body? No, sir.

418. Why not? Because I generally keep away when such occurrences are going on; they do not have anything to do with my business.

419. Then you stood in your store and saw him beaten and shot to death without attempting to interfere? I saw him shot down, and, after the first shot, heard him groan; after the second shot I do not know that I heard any noise.

420. Did you see any one in the crowd take the part of the negro? Nobody took the part of the negroes. I did not see any one take their part at all. I made the remark that it was a brutal thing at the time; that it was wrong.

422. What prevented you from going there? I knew I could do no good, and, consequently, I kept away.

Detroit, July, 1967

[From the Kerner Report, pp. 60–61.]

Of the 43 persons who were killed during the riot [Detroit], 33 were Negro and 10 were white. Seventeen were looters, of whom two were white. Fifteen citizens (of whom four were white), one white National Guardsman, one white fireman, and one Negro private guard died as the result of gunshot wounds. Most of these deaths appear to have been accidental, but criminal homicide is suspected in some.

Two persons, including one fireman, died as a result of fallen power lines. Two were burned to death. One was a drunken gunman; one an arson suspect. One white man was killed by a rioter. One police officer was felled by a shotgun blast when a gun, in the hands of another officer, accidentally discharged during a scuffle with a looter.

Action by police officers accounted for 20 and, very likely, 21 of the deaths; action by the National Guard for seven, and, very likely, nine; action by the Army for one. Two deaths were the result of action by store owners. Four persons died accidentally. Rioters were responsible for two, and perhaps three of the deaths; a private guard for one. A white man is suspected of murdering a Negro youth. The perpetrator of one of the killings in the Algiers Motel remains unknown.

Damage estimates, originally set as high as $500 million, were quickly scaled down. The city assessor's office placed the loss—excluding business stock, private furnishings, and the buildings of churches and charitable institutions—at approximately $22 million. Insurance payments, according to the State Insurance Bureau, will come to about $32 million, representing an estimated 65 to 75 per cent of the total loss.

REACTION AND RESPONSE

When the explosion subsides, and relative calm prevails, blacks are left to poke among the piles of rubble, bury their dead, and care for the wounded. After a white riot, many leave the city, and those who remain are bitter. Whites, too, survey the damage to their property and bind up their wounds, chiefly financial. They worry about their city's reputation and, after a black riot, wonder what will happen next.

Reconstruction is difficult. After the Tulsa riot, the city council passed a building code intended to preempt "Little Africa" for industrial uses, while policemen patrolled the burned-out district, arresting those who tried to rebuild houses on their own property. Only after the NAACP carried the fight to federal courts did blacks obtain relief from this form of oppression and secure the ability to protect themselves legally against the coming winter. After the black riots of the 1960s, insurance rates became prohibitive in "riot-prone" areas; bitter and insecure, many whites abandoned their former store sites. Investors were reluctant to rebuild. After all types of riots, black and white leaders formed highly visible committees to rebuild shattered race relations. Other leaders put their trust in official and private preparations for war.

Action, whether remedial or punitive, preventive or repressive, is contingent on attitudes toward the nature and causes of the riot. Whites and blacks alike have responded to white, white-black, and black riots with anger, shame, confusion, grief, and exultation. Each group tends to fault the other, regardless of the type of riot; thus, whites blame blacks for being massacred by whites, and blacks blame whites for having their stores burned by blacks. Still, neither group reacts in unison; indeed, even one man may express contradictory sentiments about these painful, bewildering outbursts.

Always, recriminations follow the trauma. It is easiest and most comforting to explain a riot as the handiwork of outside agitators who stir up the city's "riffraff"—criminals, young, hard-drinking ne'er-do-wells, unbalanced thrill-seekers—for treacherous, even treasonous, purposes. Therefore, after every riot the "better class" of citizens disclaims any connection. And finger-pointers discover sinister outside agents at work, just as Mrs. Lewis traced Nat Turner's rebellion to William Lloyd Garrison's *Liberator* in 1831. Among the "guilty" trouble makers: the Freedmen's Bureau in Memphis; the *Atlanta News* in 1906; rabble-rousing labor leaders in East St. Louis; the Bolsheviks in all the riots of 1919; the publisher of the black *Tulsa Star* and quite possibly, thought Governor Robertson, W. E. B. DuBois in Tulsa; the German Bund and the Ku Klux Klan in Detroit in 1943; and assorted communists, black power demagogues, and Martin Luther King and Stokely Carmichael in the black riots of the 1960s. This pervasive seizing on agitators reveals the reluctance of communities to believe that they have any fundamental problems and their preoccupation with the match phase of riot origins. Programs based on this reaction are likely to be merely cosmetic, punitive, and repressive.

Riots yield a peculiar blend of negative and positive short-range results. Always there is physical devastation, immediately worsened living conditions, in the black ghetto. When the riot is a black riot, this devastation can be termed a negative result; but in white and white-black riots this is a positive achievement, for the rioters intended to hurt blacks. For individuals and for the city as a whole, this destruction may be received as a challenge, as a cleansing, potentially redemptive, ritual, as an impossible obstacle, or as a sign of ultimate decay. Actual gains for rioters are common. The exodus of many blacks is in itself a positive benefit for white rioters, along with the resultant diminished black competition for jobs; such was the case in New York City, Springfield, East St. Louis, and Tulsa. Riots confer additional benefits when they provide strong arguing points for special programs. The Atlanta riot speeded the adoption of disfranchisement and helped Georgia drys secure statewide prohibition in 1907, just as the Memphis and New Orleans riots in 1866 provided telling arguments for "radical" reconstructionists interested in protecting the freedmen. The black riots of the 1960s have forced whites to notice black Americans and have opened the doors of more employers and educational institutions to more black people than had any other single cause in the previous century. Riots also enhance race consciousness, with both positive and negative consequences.

Embarrassment and concern may improve race relations at least temporarily. After Detroit's first riot, some observers noted greater public politeness, especially on crowded streetcars. Booker T. Washington noted that a black man accused of rape had been tried and proven innocent for the first time in Atlanta shortly after its riot. A

black factory worker in Detroit noticed in 1967 that his foreman
stopped cursing at him. The Springfield riot provoked responses which
led to the formation of the NAACP. Yet for all their short-range
effects, race riots have not destroyed the American caste system. It
is too early to tell whether its most serious threat—the revolt expressed
by blacks themselves in black riots—will result in its dissolution or
its reaffirmation through strict repression.

The material thus far presented has included various kinds of reactions. The attributions of causes are one form. The tone of the
narratives and comments are another. So, too, are the criticisms leveled
at the police, whom blacks have accused of inaction during white
and white-black riots and whom whites have faulted for holding back
during black riots. The selections that follow represent black and
white emotional reactions centered around approval and disapproval,
or scapegoat hunting.

Anger

In the following selections, whites react to black riots and blacks to
white riots in anger. When he heard of the Atlanta riot, W. E. B.
DuBois wrote his famous "A Litany of Atlanta." [From *The Independent* (1906) LXI, 856–58.]

A LITANY OF ATLANTA

Silent God, Thou whose voice afar in mist and mystery hath left
our ears an-hungered in these fearful days—

Hear us, good Lord!

Listen to us, Thy children: our faces dark with doubt, are
made a mockery in Thy sanctuary. With uplifted hands we front
Thy heaven, O God, crying:

We beseech Thee to hear us, good Lord!

We are not better than our fellows, Lord, we are but weak
and human men. When our devils do deviltry, curse Thou the
doer and the deed: curse them as we curse them, do to them all
and more than ever they have done to innocence and weakness, to
womanhood and home.

Have mercy upon us, miserable sinners!

And yet whose is the deeper guilt? Who made these devils?
Who nursed them in crime and fed them on injustice? Who ravished
and debauched their mothers and their grandmothers? Who bought
and sold their crime, and waxed fat and rich on public iniquity?

Thou knowest, good God!

Is this Thy justice, O Father, that guile be easier than innocence, and the innocent crucified for the guilt of the untouched guilty?

Justice, O Judge of men!

Wherefore do we pray? Is not the God of the fathers dead? Have not seers seen in Heaven's halls Thine hearsed and lifeless form stark amidst the black and rolling smoke of sin, where all along bow bitter forms of endless dead?

Awake, Thou that sleepest!

Thou art not dead, but flown afar, up hills of endless light, thru blazing corridors of suns, where worlds do swing of good and gentle men, of women strong and free—far from the cozenage, black hypocrisy and chaste prostitution of this shameful speck of dust!

Turn again, O Lord, leave us not to perish in our sin!

From lust of body and lust of blood

Great God deliver us!

From lust of power and lust of gold,

Great God deliver us!

From the leagued lying of despot and of brute,

Great God deliver us!

A city lay in travail, God our Lord, and from her loins sprang twin Murder and Black Hate. Red was the midnight; clang, crack and cry of death and fury filled the air and trembled underneath the stars when church spires pointed silently to Thee. And all this was to sate the greed of greedy men who hide behind the veil of vengeance!

Bend us Thine ear, O Lord!

In the pale, still morning we looked upon the deed. We stopped our ears and held our leaping hands, but they—did they not wag their heads and leer and cry with bloody jaws: Cease from Crime! The word was mockery, for thus they train a hundred crimes while we do cure one.

Turn again our captivity, O Lord!

Behold this maimed and broken thing; dear God it was an humble black man who toiled and sweat to save a bit from the pittance paid him. They told him: Work and Rise. He worked. Did this man sin? Nay, but some one told how some one said another did—one whom he had never seen nor known. Yet for that man's crime this man lieth maimed and murdered, his wife naked to shame, his children, to poverty and evil.

Hear us, O heavenly Father!

Doth not this justice of hell stink in Thy nostrils, O God? How long shall the mounting flood of innocent blood roar in Thine ears and pound in our hearts for vengeance? Pile the pale frenzy of blood-crazed brutes who do such deeds high on Thine altar, Jehovah Jireh, and burn it in hell forever and forever!

Forgive us, good Lord; we know not what we say!

Bewildered we are, and passion-tost, mad with the madness of a mobbed and mocked and murdered people; straining at the arm-posts of Thy Throne, we raise our shackled hands and charge Thee, God, by the bones of our stolen fathers, by the tears of our dead mothers, by the very blood of Thy crucified Christ: What Meaneth this? Tell us the Plan; give us the Sign!

Keep not thou silence, O God!

Sit no longer blind, Lord God, deaf to our prayers and dumb to our dumb suffering. Surely Thou too art not white, O Lord, a pale, bloodless, heartless thing?

Ah! Christ of all the Pities!

Forgive the thought! Forgive these wild, blasphemous words. Thou art still the God of our black fathers, and in Thy soul's soul sit some soft darkenings of the evening, some shadowings of the velvet night.

But whisper—speak—call, great God, for Thy silence is white terror to our hearts! The way, O God, show us the way and point us the path.

Whither? North is greed and South is blood; within, the coward, and without, the liar. Whither? To death?

Amen! Welcome dark sleep!

Whither? To life? But not this life, dear God, not this. Let the cup pass from us, tempt us not beyond our strength, for there is that clamoring and clawing within, to whose voice we would not listen, yet shudder lest we must, and it is red, Ah! God! It is a red and awful shape.

Selah!

In yonder East trembles a star.

Vengeance is mine; I will repay, saith the Lord!

Thy will, O Lord, be done!

Kyrie Eleison!

Lord, we have done these pleading, wavering words.

We beseech Thee to hear us, good Lord!

We bow our heads and hearken soft to the sobbing of women and little children.

We beseech Thee to hear us, good Lord!
Our voices sink in silence and in night.
Hear us, good Lord!
In night, O God of a godless land!
Amen!
In silence, O Silent God.
Selah!

Senators Russell B. Long of Louisiana and Robert C. Byrd of West Virginia reflect the anger and annoyance of whites at the continual turmoil of the 1960s. [From the *Congressional Record*, April 25, 1968.]

SENATOR LONG.

. . . If demonstrators wish to obey the law, more power to them. God bless them. If they want to express their opinions and explain what they have in mind, propose to do it peacefully, and feel that to demonstrate is the only way they can express themselves, they can do that in order to explain what their problem is. More power to them. I shall be glad to consider what they have in mind.

But, Mr. President, the people of this country are getting enough of that kind of thinking that lets our Government be run by rioters.

I do not believe that there is any State in the Union where a majority of the people would vote to support the philosophy of the Kerner Commission report, that we should give the rioters and the lawbreakers what they demand and maybe they will quit breaking the law.

Mr. President, every mother in America knows that will not work. Every mother knows that if a child misbehaves and is not corrected, possibly chastised, and made to realize he did wrong and to feel repentant about it, that child will continue to misbehave.

To reward a child for making mischief is only to make a bad child.

It is somewhat parallel to the proverb "spare the rod and spoil the child." A child must be taught to behave.

The same thing is true of the criminal element in this country. They must be taught to obey the law. While it is true that some of them have just cause for complaint, if they do not stay within the bounds of propriety, those who would sympathize with them, cannot and should not give the time, help, and support they would give otherwise.

❋   ❋   ❋

MR. BYRD of West Virginia.

. . . Let me say, with regard to the shooting of rioters, it has been the law that a policeman is under a duty to arrest anyone who commits a felony. He may use whatever force is necessary to make and maintain that arrest. He is also under a duty, if he cannot make and maintain the arrest, to prevent the escape of the felon and he can use whatever force is necessary in order to prevent the escape of that felon. He may shoot a fleeing felon in order to prevent his escape if all other means have been exhausted.

Riot or no riot, that is the law.

When an individual heaves a Molotov cocktail into a building and sets that building on fire, that is arson. It is a felony.

When an individual heaves a brick through a store window, enters the store and makes off with stolen goods, that is burglary. It is a felony.

A policeman is under a duty to prevent the escape of a fleeing felon. If he cannot prevent the escape in any other way, after all other means have been exhausted, then he may shoot that felon.

There has been a great furor about what Mayor Daley said.

I am on Mayor Daley's side.

I do not care who in this town takes issue with him. I do not care what office that individual in this town may hold, or how high up it may be. I think that Mayor Daley was merely stating the law. He was expressing a greater concern for the victims of felons and for future victims than for the fleeing felon. In my judgment, he stated the right priority. I called Mayor Daley yesterday on the telephone to commend him on his stand.

Mr. President, I am tired and the law-abiding public is tired of this pussyfooting by the Attorney General of the United States—who recently clashed with Mayor Daley—or by anyone else. Name him— I am tired of it, and the American people are tired of it.

I wonder when our leaders in Washington are going to come to their senses and take a firm, unequivocal, unmistakable, and strong stand against rioters and all those who commit acts of violence. Such a stand is long overdue. Of course a policeman should not shoot a child. Of course a policeman should not shoot into a crowd. But when a curfew has been instituted, as it was here in Washington—and it was effectively instituted—the criminal element should be warned, that if they persist in rioting and committing acts of violence, they will do so at the risk of life and limb. And then, if they persist, let the criminal element suffer the consequences.

The criminal element understand one language, and understands it well—and that is the language of force. No criminal is afraid of a gun that is not loaded or of a policeman or soldier who is under orders not to shoot.

Mr. President, I do not want to see loss of life any more than any other high official of this Government wants to see loss of life; but I say it is up to the criminal element. They know the law; let the warning be issued. If they fail to heed it, let them suffer the consequences.

Government has a right to survive. Law-abiding people are entitled to protection of their lives and properties.

The first duty of government is to enforce the law and preserve order. This is the first priority, for without order there can be no liberty—only anarchy. Without law, there can be no rule of reason—only tyranny.

Shame

Expressions of shame condemning a riot by members of one's own race have not been plentiful among spokesmen in a riot city; such sentiments usually come from outside. The *Memphis Commercial-Appeal* here bathes Atlanta in shame. [Reprinted in *Atlanta Constitution*, September 26, 1906.]

Shame to the South

Unlike other sections of the country, where the principle seems to be to shoot all negroes when one of them has excited public fury, in the south the unwritten law declares death for the guilty alone; pacification and protection for the innocent. Atlanta, with its reckless rioting, its bullets for every black face and its stones and sticks for all black bodies, has reproduced Chicago scenes in the south, overthrown whatever of justice there may have been in lynch law, and applied a cleaver to that bond of confidence which the innocent negro of the south felt in the justice of the white man of this section. . . . No wonder patience and self-control were lost; but in the losing of these virtues and the resulting desperate rioting, however great the provocation, Atlanta brought shame to the south, and has set a fuse that is more than apt to cause a most harrowing explosion.

[The black *Michigan Chronicle* carried this editorial, "Vandalism," on July 3, 1943, following the Detroit riot of that year.]

There is an old American adage which has been worn thin by repetition but which we believe should be profoundly impressed upon everyone of us in the Negro community of Detroit. It runs, "two wrongs do not make a right." We have charged the Detroit police with brutality and downright savagery. We have blasted and condemned the Klan-minded gutterpups who take an inhuman delight in crucifying men, women and children simply because they were born black. We shall continue to demand that these foul elements in our society be eliminated as long as there is breath left in us.

Nevertheless, we challenge any sane Negro citizen to tour the commercial streets in our district and come away feeling that the devastation and ruin created by people of our own group reflect credit upon us. The horrifying destruction of property and wanton looting cannot be defended by any person who has an ounce of integrity and self-respect. We know that only a small minority of Negroes participated in this frightful pillage but it only takes a minority among us to defeat the very ends which the whole race wants and demands.

While we do not share the Uncle Tom views which insist that we must take oppression lying down with only a prayer on our lips, we cannot condone savagery among ourselves any more than we do among other groups. If we have grievances against white shopkeepers in our district, there are many far more effective ways of expressing them than wanton looting. We can still spend our money where we choose.

It is our earnest hope that the Negro leadership takes cognizance of what happened last week. To say that we are oppressed and are the products of the slums created by the whites who detest us cannot absolve us of our rightful responsibilities for maintaining civilized behavior. Furthermore by such savagery not a single gain has been won and on the other hand we tend to alienate many who are willing to join us in a decent, democratic struggle for the rights and privileges which we demand. The truth must be told even if it may be temporarily unpopular.

Former president William Howard Taft blamed whites for the riot in Tulsa. [From the *Tulsa Tribune,* June 13, 1921.]

No matter whether it was a negro or a white man who began the initial fight, one cannot escape the conclusion that the awful character of this cruel massacre was largely due to the outrageous malevolence and cruelty of the whites who took part in the conflict.

This is clearly indicated by the number of negro dead as compared with the dead whites, by the wholesale destruction and looting of the negro settlement and business quarter, by the fact that white men prevented the effort of the city fire department to put out the flames and by the present suffering and homelessness of the thousands of negroes of Tulsa.

This conclusion does not excuse, of course the propaganda which some negro papers are pressing among their readers, inciting them to physical force in the assertion of their equality of right and fanning their passion and their fears by detailed recital of wrongs to negroes in every part of the country. Race pride and confidence in the prowess of negro veterans of the late war have been stirred to aid the incitement.

*   *   *

It is a disgrace to our civilization, and everything possible should be done to prevent another such shameful and brutal exhibition. In a country in which we boast of constitutions securing the life, liberty and property of every individual we must blush at such a gross and demoralizing departure from our ideals, and should be profoundly moved to take effective measures to prevent its recurrence.

Riots Can Only Hurt the Cause

Whites often warn blacks that the use of force will cost them white goodwill and jeopardize their cause. [From J. E. McCulloch (General Secretary, Southern Sociological Congress), Washington, to the Editor, *The Outlook,* September 3, 1919, p. 28, after the Washington riot, 1919.]

Nothing is more foolish than for the Negro to fight for his rights, for the more he fights the further the procession of American civilization moves ahead. He forgets that he has absolutely nothing that the white man will turn back in the procession to get—no language, no literature, no commerce, no art, no science, no philosophy, no religion. The destiny of the Negro in America is as inexorable as the law of gravitation. He must advance or perish, and he can advance only by winning the good will of the great white hosts ahead of him.

The Injury of Innocents

[Editorial, *The Dallas Morning News,* August 14, 1965, following the 1965 riot in Los Angeles.]

The tragedy of the senseless riots in a Negro section of Los Angeles is that they will hurt innocent people who had nothing to do with the violence.

California has perhaps as little racial discrimination as any state in the Union. If anything, the law and courts lean in the other direction. Public accommodations are integrated; there are no racial bars to voting or jobs.

Yet thousands of Negroes have gathered in the Watts area of Los Angeles recently to stage deliberate race riots. They have run wild, burning cars, beating up motorists, looting stores. There was no justification or even reason for such behavior. It was, as a police spokesman said, "rebellion against authority . . . any authority."

But the greatest damage inflicted by the mobs is to the hundreds of thousands of decent, law-abiding Negroes who live in Los Angeles. Lawless behavior of this sort, by focusing anger and fear on the Negro race, helps to perpetuate what civil-rights groups call de facto segregation.

De facto segregation, unlike segregation by law, is the result of decision by individuals. It cannot be eliminated by marches, sit-ins or bloc voting. It occurs when Negro families move into a neighborhood and the white families move out. Antisocial behavior of the type displayed in Los Angeles is a big factor in causing whites to make the decision.

Obviously this situation is unfair to Negroes who are as responsible citizens as their new neighbors. Decent Negroes are no more to blame for the Negro mobs than are decent whites for the riots staged by white punks. But the situation does exist and attempts of some civil-rights leaders to excuse lawlessness by mobs or by individuals or to blame it on history or society do not improve matters.

Most whites still believe that the individual is responsible for his actions, that if a man takes to the streets to commit arson and assault he, and not society, is to blame. This belief is logical.

Unfortunately many hold the less-logical belief that the man's race is also somehow to blame, if he is of a different minority. Illogical or not, the belief is widely held and it is today one of the chief obstructions to real integration.

This being the case, it would seem that those who hope to end de facto segregation might help their cause best by working to prevent antisocial actions within their own race instead of seeking scapegoats in government or "power structures." Such actions are doing far greater injury to their cause than anything done by white-supremacy groups.

The Messenger, a black journal, was furious at hearing Negro leaders scold blacks for having fought in Chicago and Washington in 1919. [From "Negro Leaders Compromise as Usual," *The Messenger*, September, 1919.]

In Washington, during the riot, it was Judge Robert Terrell and Emmet J. Scott who led the inglorious compromise as usual. Those two would-be leaders issued a joint letter, in which they said "the retaliation which followed the attack of the white mob on the part of colored people was to be deplored." In Chicago, Illinois, another compromise Negro leader outdid Scott, Terrell and Robert Russa Moton in the sycophancy and spinelessness of his advice and observation. We refer to Beauregard F. Moseley. This hand picked Negro said:

"Some of us forget that the white man has given us freedom, the right to vote, to live on terms of equality with him, to be paid well for our work and to receive many other benefits. Now, if the white man should decide that the black man has proved he is not fit to have the right to vote, that right might be taken away, we might also find it difficult to receive other favors to which we have been accustomed, and then what would happen to us?

"We must remember that this is a white man's country. Without his help we can do nothing. When we fight the white man we fight ourselves. We can start a riot, but it takes the white man to stop it. We are interested not in what started the riots but how to stop them."

May we ask what our readers think of this observation of one Beauregard Moseley? Just what did he get for making this statement and what white men were fools enough to believe that his statements would have the slightest effect among the New Negroes of this country, except to pour oil on the fire? The white man has not given us any freedom, neither the northern nor the southern man. What we have gotten we have taken, and such concessions as have been granted were granted merely because they were beneficial to him. The right to vote was granted to the Negro in the South during the Reconstruction days because a group of hypocritical, reactionary and plutocratic Republicans wanted to keep in power in order that they might control the granting of franchises, the selling of privileges to railroads, the stealing of coal lands, plundering the public domain and, above all, because they would have the power to lay and collect taxes on everybody while exempting themselves. They found Negroes to be efficient tools in helping them maintain this power. But just so soon as those Republican hypocrites, represented by this same Chicago Tribune, were able to see their way clear to election in the North and West, without the aid of the Southern Negroes, the Southern Negroes were gracefully turned over to the tender mercies of their former white masters. What happened since is a matter of history. The story of disfranchisement, grandfather clauses, the Ku-Klux-Klan and lynching is familiar to every child of seven years of age. Moseley ought to know that most Negroes do not enjoy their right to vote. We are now fighting to live on terms of equality with the white man, which shows on its face that we do not enjoy the right. To be paid well for our work is far away from any actuality. . . .

Moseley says that we must remember that this is a white man's country. Well, we have fought like hell for it and unless we get part of it and enjoy it peacefully we will riot all over the United States. And as we proceed in our fight for it, a black rascal and a sniveling scoundrel, who betrays the trust of the toiling black workers, will fare no better than a white scoundrel, and probably a little bit worse. Why even white men no longer talk about this being a white man's country, unless it be Hoke Smith, Vardaman, John Sharp Williams, Cole Blease or some such Southern bourbon. This hand picked Negro also says: "We can start a riot, but it takes the white man to stop it." Where does he get this interpretation? The evidence shows that in Washington and Chicago, the whites started the riots, but it took the Negroes to stop them. Had it not been for Negro self-assertion and manhood, the riot sport would have proceeded until white men got tired and stopped of their own free will. But not so of recent date. The Negroes took the defensive-offensive in Washington, and according to the papers, the move was marked "by general preparedness on the part of the Negroes." Chicago would have been another East St. Louis except for the Negroes stopping the rioters.

Exultation

While anger, shame, and disapproval are common reactions, so are expressions of pleasure. Rioters, or those who see rioters as their own representatives in a cause, exult over the psychological and strategical gains they perceive will follow the riot. In the next selection, whites gloat over a white riot. [Editorial, *Memphis Avalanche,* May 5, 1866; reprinted in *Memphis Riots and Massacres,* p. 334.]

The late riots in our city have satisfied all of one thing: that the southern men will not be ruled by the negro. For months past acts of violence, bloodshed and murder have been too common; but they have almost always had some direct connexion with the negro troops stationed here. Time and again stores have been broken open and plundered, and white men shot down in our city by drunken, brutal negro soldiers; and we have yet to hear of the first instance where punishment followed the crime. We readily grant that it was often, in fact almost always, impossible to identify the offenders, as the crimes were generally committed after dark. We only speak of the facts, however; and, believing that negro troops were the prime cause, our citizens again and again petitioned that they should be removed. In all these cases of violence the officers of the law had been left to vindicate the law and protect the rights of the people, whose peace and quiet they are sworn to protect. The citizens themselves took no part in all these altercations, and hence the negro soldiers began to believe that they could manage things their own way. This idea of insolence culminated on Tuesday evening, and they became engaged in a fatal altercation with the police. Then, for the first time, our citizens took part in the fight; and the negroes now know, to their sorrow, that it is best not to arouse the fury of the white man.

Black poet Claude McKay in 1919 captured the defiance and manliness of the "New Negro" in a sonnet inspired by demonstrations of black willingness to fight when faced with white riots. [Claude McKay, "If We Must Die." Reprinted by permission of Twayne Publishers, Inc.]

IF WE MUST DIE

If we must die—let it not be like hogs
Hunted and penned in an inglorious spot.
While round us bark the mad and hungry dogs,
Making their mock at our accursed lot.
If we must die—oh, let us nobly die,
So that our precious blood may not be shed
In vain; then even the monsters we defy
Shall be constrained to honor us though dead!
Oh, Kinsmen! We must meet the common foe;
Though far outnumbered, let us show us brave,
And for their thousand blows deal one death-blow!
What though before us lies the open grave?
Like men we'll face the murderous, cowardly pack,
Pressed to the wall, dying, but fighting back!

On Watts

Below, a black glories in black riot. [From Eldridge Cleaver, *Soul On Ice* (New York: McGraw-Hill, Inc., 1968; London: Jonathan Cape Limited), pp. 26–27. Copyright 1968 by Eldridge Cleaver. Reprinted by permission of the publishers.]

Folsom Prison
August 16, 1965

As we left the Mess Hall Sunday morning and milled around in the prison yard, after four days of abortive uprising in Watts, a group of low riders from Watts assembled on the basketball court. They were wearing jubilant, triumphant smiles, animated by a vicarious spirit by which they, too, were in the thick of the uprising taking place hundreds of miles away to the south in the Watts ghetto.

"Man," said one, "what they doing out there? Break it down for me, Baby."

They slapped each other's outstretched palms in a cool salute and burst out laughing with joy.

"Home boy, them Brothers is taking care of Business!" shrieked another ecstatically.

Then one low rider, stepping into the center of the circle formed by the others, rared back on his legs and swaggered, hunching his belt up with his forearms as he'd seen James Cagney and George Raft do in too many gangster movies. I joined the circle. Sensing a creative moment in the offing, we all got very quiet, very still, and others passing by joined the circle and did likewise.

"Baby," he said, "They walking in fours and kicking in doors; dropping Reds and busting heads; drinking wine and committing crime, shooting and looting; high-siding and low-riding, setting fires and slashing tires; turning over cars and burning down bars; making Parker mad and making me glad; putting an end to that 'go slow' crap and putting sweet Watts on the map—my black ass is in Folsom this morning but my black heart is in Watts!" Tears of joy were rolling from his eyes.

It was a cleansing, revolutionary laugh we all shared, something we have not often had occasion for.

Watts was a place of shame. We used to use Watts as an epithet in much the same way as city boys used "country" as a term of derision. To deride one as a "lame," who did not know what was happening (a rustic bumpkin), the "in-crowd" of the time from L.A. would bring a cat down by saying that he had just left Watts, that he ought to go back to Watts until he had learned what was happening, or that he had just stolen enough money to move out of Watts and was already trying to play a cool part. But now, blacks are seen in Folsom saying, "I'm from Watts, Baby!"—whether true or not, but I think their meaning is clear. Confession: I, too, have participated in this game, saying, I'm from Watts. In fact, I did live there for a time, and I'm *proud* of it, the tired lamentations of Whitney Young, Roy Wilkins, and The Preacher notwithstanding.

Here, a white honors white rioters. [W. A. Bainster, Tulsa, Okla., to the Editor, *The Tulsa Tribune*, June 10, 1921.]

After accepting your array of statements in your editorial of Sunday morning as facts, and after reading the admission of guilt by every negro, referred to in the Sunday sermons as reported in this morning's World, I wish to ask are we a city of "negro-philes," and why not one word of sympathy was or has been expressed for the dead "white-whites" whose lives lost, homes blighted and relatives plunged in grief, seventy-five or one hundred white, shedding their red blood, and offering their lives, if need be (a truly vicarious sacrifice) that their firesides might be freed from the black menace, the high sheriff of this county told them he was powerless to stay; and through a night of horror and morn of strife and blood shed were borne to couches of pain and suffering, upheld by no hope of a grateful peoples' pension and praise, but by the lone thought "He had done what he could," and the Negro-philes execrating their heroism, their suffering, and pitying the criminal coon, because they were not able to expend their arsenal church supplies on these, and all other white-white home defenders. Will some white-white minister at sometime, some-where, lay a small posey on the graves of these white-white dead, and speak a word of cheer to the wounded white-whites for their valued defense of law and order.

I have ever taught my children that there could never be negro equality as long as the M. E. church, South, functioned, but from this morning's paper, even its highest exponent is on the run. Nigger-town is gone forever and they will not settle in a graveyard, but will some white-white not a negro-phile, with red blood in his veins, say a short prayer for our white-white dead, murmur a blessing for a white injured, and announce to the world that there is yet a remnant of white-whites in Tulsa sufficient at least for the needs of the hour.

Who will be the first white-white minister with enough red blood in his veins to shrive the blood or the white-white martyrs. He might murmur "These too have not striven in vain."

"We Deplore This Outburst, But . . ."

Both white and black spokesmen have responded to white and black riots, respectively, by deploring the excesses of the explosion.

But their message may in fact constitute a warning that the riot will be repeated if causal conditions are not remedied. This tends to vitiate the opening note of condemnation. Below, a white warning after a white riot. [From editorial, "Race Riots on the Streets Last Night the Inevitable Result of a Carnival of Crime Against Our White Women," *Atlanta News*, September 23, 1906.]

The News does not indorse the disorder which occurred during the evening, but we say it was the inevitable result and effect of the terrible deeds committed by the blacks in this community in recent weeks, and especially on yesterday.

No wonder the minds of the white men were inflamed at these repeated outrages.

The wonder is that the white men did not begin in earnest a real warfare against the blacks.

If these crimes continue, this conflict is coming, and coming soon, and preparations may as well be made for it.

The News urges citizens to restrain themselves and keep their heads cool.

A serious time has come upon us.

It is no time for excitement or passion.

Serious work must be done and men should be in possession of their best judgment and restrain themselves so that wise but certain action may be taken.

If it comes to the worst, we may as well be prepared to handle the situation promptly and effectively.

Orderly, law-abiding negroes should remain at their homes and be quiet until the excitement of yesterday and last night dies down.

They should refrain from making insulting or vicious remarks among themselves and within the hearing of the whites.

Their impudence and impertinence will not be tolerated.

The white men are furious at the crimes which have been committed by the lustful devils of the community and they are in a frame of mind where they will make the innocent suffer as well as the guilty if occasion requires.

The slightest demonstration of impudence or resentment on the part of the negroes will be promptly punished by the whites.

White men should be calm and not provoke conflicts with the blacks.

The News believes in recognizing and speaking the truth.

It may as well be said, then, that the race war has begun.

Let no man misunderstand the cause and beginning of the conflict.

Many of the defenseless white women of this community have been shamefully outraged and viciously assaulted.

It is no wonder the white men have started to avenge these crimes and protect their homes and their wives and children, from the awful fate which has befallen many of the white women.

We prefer peace and order, but if it must be war, the white men are ready to face it.

Go to the cause and condemn the crimes of these vicious negroes against our white women.

Stop the assault and the outrages and there will be no riots and no disorder and no race conflicts in this community.

The News stands for and believes in law and order, but in the name of Heaven, what else can white men do except to make war to the bitter end against the black devils who continue to ravish defenseless white women, and who are destroying one home after another and wrecking the lives and the hopes of many of the white women of this county!

> Almost sixty years later, a black warning after a black riot. ["Jackie Robinson Says: 'Out of The Ashes Someone Better Learn New Negro,'" *Pittsburgh Courier,* August 28, 1965.]

We are unequivocally opposed to looting under the pretense of participating in violent protest.

We are unequivocally opposed to violent protest.

We are as unequivocally against black hatred as we are against white hatred.

But—and that is a terribly big but—we refuse to be silent when the terrible and destructive action of hoodlums and exploiters and hate-crazed saboteurs is used as an argument that the Negro doesn't know how to wear the new clothes of freedom which are finally being offered to him to cover the nakedness in which he has been shivering for 300 years.

Much is being made of the fact that the outbreak in Los Angeles occurred virtually simultaneously with the passing of the Voting Rights Bill. This coincidence, if coincidence it was, furnished grist for the propaganda mills of the Faubuses and the Wallaces. But, for intelligent and reasoning people, this coincidence does not mean that the Negro is being given too much. In fact, there may be some merit in the assumption that the very irony of the necessity to pass such a bill after so long an era of denial, is sufficient to arouse the wrath of many Negro people.

We are not condoning the method in which this wrath was expressed on the West Coast in recent days.

The massive police power invoked to quell the lawlessness which took place was necessary.

Yet the past use of police power in that city—as in many other cities—has been abuse of police power where the Negro has been concerned. If rioting is to be prevented in the future, Mayor Yorty and Governor Brown and Chief Parker (preferably a new police chief) will have to face that fact.

There are other facts which must be faced, not only in ravaged California but all throughout the land.

There is the fact that the civil rights leadership may no longer be regarded as the magic password to insure racial peace between black and white in America. The grass roots Negro in many communities, the individual we call the man on the street, is no longer excited or soothed because Mr. Big Negro Leader is welcomed to City Hall. He is no longer excited about a few big jobs being passed around. Because the law of the land took so long to heed Roy Wilkins and Thurgood Marshall in their suit for justice, because the rulers of the land took so long to endorse the non-violent tactics of Martin Luther King; because industry took so long to understand the common-sense advice of Lester Granger and Whitney Young; because of all this— a new Negro is striding the land. He is unafraid to die. He is intolerant of the virtues of patience. He sees massive forces being sent to Vietnam by a Government which cries that it cannot protect black and white patriots who journey South on missions of democracy. He is not—in the main—an advocate of offensive violence like that which took place in Los Angeles. But he loves the Deacons for justice who don't slap first, nor will he turn the other cheek.

Someone—many someones—better learn how to speak the language of this new Negro. The power structure of the cities and the states and the Federal Government better get the message which burns in the hearts of this new Negro. The civil rights leadership will have to learn how to communicate with him better, and they can start by learning how to communicate with each other better.

Riffraff and Agitators

After riots of all types the good citizens disavowed any involvement. According to them, rioters represented only the "lower elements" of the city's population. [O. W. Gurley, Negro hotel proprietor, *Tulsa Tribune*, June 4, 1921.]

There were not more than 40 to 50 men in the crowd of armed blacks who marched upon the courthouse. They were nearly all dope users or "jake" drinkers with police records. . . . I am telling the whole truth so far as I know it because I, in common with all good colored citizens of Tulsa, which includes by far the larger number of the negroes, want those men of our race who armed themselves and marched on the courthouse punished. They started the trouble and this fellow Mann fired the first shot. They brought calamity on us when we were doing our best to make good.

[Editorial, *Dallas Morning News*, August 14, 1965.]

Decent Negroes are no more to blame for the Negro mobs than are decent whites for the riots staged by white punks.

[Editorial, *Detroit News*, June 23, 1943.]

We must keep in mind the kind of people we have to deal with in this connection. They are half-baked, half-educated people—white and colored alike.

[Dr. A. R. Holderby, Presbyterian minister, *Atlanta Constitution*, September 24, 1906.]

I am of course sorry it occurred, as is every law-abiding citizen, . . .

[Resolution of mass meeting, *Atlanta Constitution*, September 26, 1906.]

We deplore the crimes of both races which have been committed by their worst elements, . . .

[Witness John Martin, *Memphis Riots and Massacres*, p. 137]

And in connexion with that I may say I have not seen any respectable gentleman who did not deprecate this thing.

[Witness Marland H. Perkins, *Memphis Riots and Massacres*, p. 289.]

I never heard a respectable man in the city of Memphis express anything but the most profound regret at the occurrence.

4753. Were the acts of the mob universally condemned? Universally. I never heard a man of intelligence express a contrary opinion.

[Investigating Chairman, Elihu Washbourne, *Memphis Riots and Massacres*, p. 290.]

4775. You have spoken of the people of Memphis and of their good treatment of the colored people; and kindness to them; who was it that burned the colored school-houses and churches of Memphis, on the 1st and 2nd of May? Who was it that set fire to the houses, and attempted to burn up the inmates? Who was it that robbed the colored people? Who was it that ravished the women? Who was it that shot down women and children in cold blood?

[Editorial, *Harper's Weekly*, August 1, 1863.]

Some newspapers dwell upon the fact that the rioters were uniformly Irish, and hence argue that our trouble arises from the perversity of the Irish race. But how do these theorists explain the fact that riots precisely similar to that of last week have occurred within our time at Paris, Madrid, Naples, Rome, Berlin, and Vienna; and that the Lord George Gordon riots in London, before our time, far surpassed our New York riot in every circumstance of atrocity? Turbulence is no exclusive attribute of the Irish character: it is common to all mobs in all countries. It happens in this city that, in our working classes, the Irish element largely preponderates over all others, and if the populace acts as a populace Irishmen are naturally prominent therein. It happens, also, that from the limited opportunities which the Irish enjoy for education in their own country, they are more easily mislead by knaves, and made the tools of politicians, when they come here, than Germans or men of other races. The impulsiveness of the Celt, likewise, prompts him to be foremost in every outburst, whether for a good or for an evil purpose. But it must be remembered, in palliation of the disgrace which, as Archbishop Hughes says, the riots of last week have heaped upon the Irish name, that in many wards of the city the Irish were during the late riot stanch friends of law and order; that Irishmen helped to rescue the colored orphans in the asylum from the hands of the rioters; that a large proportion of the police, who behaved throughout the riot with the most exemplary gallantry, are Irishmen; that the Roman Catholic priesthood to a man used their influence on the side of the law; and that perhaps the most scathing rebuke administered to the riot was written by an Irishman—James T. Brady.

Researchers supplementing the work of the Kerner Commission examined the "riffraff theory" of participation in black riots. [From Robert M. Fogelson and Robert B. Hill, "Who Riots? A Study of Participation in the 1967 Riots," *Supplemental Studies for the National Advisory Commission on Civil Disorders*, pp. 221–23, 231, 237–38, 242–43.]

Their answer is what we refer to as the "riffraff theory" of riot participation. At the core of this "theory" are three distinct, though closely related, themes. First, that only an infinitesimal fraction of the black population (2 per cent according to some, including several prominent Negro moderates, and 1 per cent according to others) actively participated in the riots. Second, that the rioters, far from being representative of the Negro community, were principally the riffraff—the unattached, juvenile, unskilled, unemployed, uprooted, criminal—and outside agitators. Indeed, many public figures have insisted that outside agitators, especially left-wing radicals and black nationalists, incited the riffraff and thereby provoked the rioting. And third, that the overwhelming majority of the Negro population—the law-abiding and respectable 98 or 99 per cent who did not join the rioting—unequivocally opposed and deplored the riots.

For most white Americans the riffraff theory is highly reassuring. If, indeed, the rioters were a tiny fraction of the Negro population, composed of the riffraff and outside agitators and opposed by a large majority of the ghetto residents, the riots were less ominous than they appeared. They were also a function of poverty, which, in American ideology, is alterable, rather than race, which is immutable; in which case too, they were peripheral to the issue of white-black relations in the United States. Again if the riffraff theory is correct, the riots were a reflection less of the social problems of modern black ghettos than of the personal disabilities of recent Negro newcomers. And the violent acts—the looting, arson, and assault—were not political protests, but rather, in the words of the McCone Commission, "formless, quite senseless," and by implication, "meaningless" outbursts. Lastly, if the prevailing view of riot participation is accurate, future riots can be prevented merely elevating the riffraff, and by muzzling outside agitators, without transforming the black ghettos. Without, in other words, radically changing the American metropolis by thoroughly overhauling its basic institutions or seriously inconveniencing its white majority.

In view of the profound implications of the riffraff theory, it is disconcerting that very few of its adherents have offered solid supporting evidence. Their estimates of participation were based largely on the impressions of subordinates, who had good reason to play down the rioting, and not on interviews with lower-class and working-class Negroes. Their descriptions of the rioters were drawn primarily from personal observations and, in a handful of cases, casual, and often poorly informed, glances at arrest statistics. Their opinions about ghetto attitudes were formed mainly from cursory soundings of moderate Negroes, who strongly opposed the rioting, and not of militant blacks. The adherents of the riffraff theory have also overlooked a good deal of evidence which sharply questions and sometimes directly contradicts their position. For example, unless the police caught most of the rioters—which is highly unlikely—the large number of arrests alone indicates that more than 1 or 2 per cent of the Negroes participated. The written and graphic descriptions of the riots reveal that many working- and middle-class blacks joined in the looting and assaults (if not the burning). And the remarks of Negroes during and after the rioting suggest that many who did not themselves participate tacitly supported the rioters anyway.

Why, then, has the riffraff theory been so widely adopted to explain the 1960's riots? Why was it adopted to explain the Harlem riots of 1935 and 1943 and many earlier riots in America as well? The answer, we believe, can be traced to the American conviction that no matter how grave the grievances there are no legitimate grounds for violent protest—a conviction shared by most whites that reflect the nation's traditional confidence in orderly social change. To have accepted the possibility that a substantial and representative segment of the Negro population participated in or supported the riots would have forced most Americans to draw one of two conclusions. Either that the long-term deterioration of the black ghettos has destroyed the prospect for gradual improvement and provided the justification for violent protest, or that even if conditions are not so desperate a great many Negroes believe otherwise. Neither conclusion could have been reconciled with the commitment to orderly social change; either one would have compelled most Americans to re-examine a fundamental feature of the ideology of their race, class, and country. And, not surprisingly, they were no more inclined to do so than previous generations of Americans.

*   *   *

In sum, we have found that many of the social traits predicted by the second component of the riffraff theory to characterize rioters were over-represented among the arrestees, and in some instances, decidedly so. Much of this, of course, was due to the biases of the arrest data. But "over-representativeness" is quite a different matter from saying that the arrestees had predominantly riffraff characteristics. In spite of the heavy over-representation of young, single males, the striking facts are—again in view of the historic efficacy of the customary re-

straints on rioting in the United States, especially among Negroes—
that one-half to three-quarters of the arrestees were employed in semi-
skilled or skilled occupations, three-fourths were employed, and three-
tenths to six-tenths were born outside the South. So to claim, as the
second point of the riffraff theory does, that the rioters were principally the riffraff and outside agitators—rather than fairly typical
young Negroe [sic] males—is to seriously misconstrue the 1960's riots.

❋   ❋   ❋

These surveys indicate that, in addition to the large number of people who felt the riots were inevitable, a large minority or a small
majority of the Negro community regards them as beneficial, essential.
According to the Institute of Government and Public Affairs, moreover, the Negroes in Los Angeles objected to the rioting mainly on
pragmatic rather than principled grounds; they disapproved of the
violent consequences of the riots rather than the riots themselves.
Whereas 29 per cent disliked the burning and 19 per cent the looting,
21 per cent protested the shooting and the killing and 13 per cent the
police action, and only 1 per cent objected to the Negro rioting and
1 per cent to the Negro assault. According to the Institute of Government and Public Affairs, too, the relatively well-to-do and well-edu-
cated supported the Los Angeles riots as much as the less well-off and
poorly-educated, though, according to the University of Michigan's
Survey Research Center, the counter-rioters in Detroit tended to be
more affluent and better educated than the rioters. And according to
the Harris organization, lower- and lower-middle-income Negroes were
somewhat more likely to regard the riots favorably than middle- and
upper-middle-income Negroes; and Negroes 34 years and younger
were considerably more likely to do so than Negroes 50 years and
older and even more than Negroes between the ages of 35 and 49.

These findings are consistent with the impressionistic accounts of
the 1960s riots. The first-hand descriptions of the riots and the on-the-
spot interviews with ghetto residents revealed a great deal of tacit
support for the rioters among the non-rioters. Apparently many of
them also saw the rioting as a protest, and a successful one at that,
against the grievances of the Negro ghettos—a protest which, if need
be, would be delivered again. Their feelings were well articulated by
a middle-age Negro woman who ran an art gallery in southcentral Los
Angeles: "I will not take a Molotov cocktail," she said, "but I am as
mad as they (the rioters) are." Nor are these findings inconsistent with
a commonsense approach to the 1960s riots. After all, is it conceivable
that (as the third point of the riffraff theory holds) several hundred
riots could have erupted in nearly every Negro ghetto in the United
States over the past five years against the opposition of 98 or 99 per

cent of the black community? And is it conceivable that militant young
Negroes would have ignored the customary restraints on rioting in
the United States, including the commitment to orderly social change,
unless they enjoyed the tacit support of at least a sizable minority of
the black community?

If the survey research, arrest data, and impressionistic accounts are
indicative, the rioters were a small but significant minority of the
Negro population, fairly representative of the ghetto residents, and
especially of the young adult males, and tacitly supported by at least
a large minority of the black community. Which, to repeat, means that
the 1960s riots were a reflection of the social problems of modern
black ghettos, a protest against the essential conditions of life there,
and an indicator of the necessity for fundamental changes in American
society. And if the riffraff theory has not been accurate in the past, its
accuracy in the future is seriously questioned.

Scapegoat Hunting, Detroit, 1943

Outside agitators have been blamed for virtually every race riot.
The following selections present a case study of some of the attempts
to spot the perpetrators of the Detroit riot of 1943. [Col. Fred Sullem,
publisher of Jackson, Miss., *Daily News,* quoted in *Michigan Chronicle,* July 3, 1943.]

It is blood on your hands, Mrs. Eleanor Roosevelt.

More than any other person, you are morally responsible for those
race riots in Detroit where two dozen were killed and fully 500 injured in nearly a solid day of street fighting.

You have been personally proclaiming and practicing social equality
at the White House and wherever you go, Mrs. Roosevelt.

In Detroit, a city noted for the growing impudence and insolence
of its Negro population an attempt was made to put your preach-
ments into practice, Mrs. Roosevelt.

Blood on your hand, Mrs. Roosevelt. And the damned spot won't
wash out, either.

[Statement by white civic leaders, Detroit, printed in *Detroit News,*
June 22, 1943.]

Detroit is today the scene of outrageous violations of civic peace
and national unity. National unity is endangered. War production is
partially paralyzed.

This is not an isolated incident arising from a chance fist-fight, but is part of an organized national fifth column conspiracy to break our national unity and disrupt the home production front.

The overwhelming majority of Detroiters are loyal Americans who want no part of these enemy-aiding disturbances. We want to see good relations between all Americans and a united war effort.

We therefore call upon Mayor Jeffries, Gov. Kelly and the Federal Government to restore order and punish those responsible for the outbreaks by:

Clearly and publicly placing the blame where it belongs—on the Axis-hiding Ku Klux Klan and other fifth column elements in Detroit who have created this situation.

Immediate roundup and arrest of all known Klan and other fifth column leaders and followers in the Detroit area.

Adequate protection for all citizens and immediate removal of any police and other officers who are guilty of collusion with those responsible for the attacks upon the Negro people.

Immediate discontinuance of closing of schools and curtailing of transportation and other acts which only add to panic and confusion and further disrupt war production.

We call upon every patriotic white Detroit citizen:

Not to believe or spread false anti-Negro rumors. The rumor of a Negro uprising, and rumors of attacks by Negroes are Axis-inspired lies for the purpose of frightening white Americans into unjust and ill-considered action which harms the war effort.

Help defeat the purpose of this fifth column outrage by maintaining civic peace and discipline and the normal flow of war production. Maintain unity in the shop.

Above all to maintain full national unity with our colored brothers and all other American minority groups so that the fifth column outburst shall fail, and our country shall go forward resolutely to victory over the Axis.

[Hon. John E. Rankin, Miss., *Congressional Record—Appendix,* July 1, 1943, p. A3630.]

It is dawning on the American people who is creating and promoting this race trouble and these race riots throughout the country.

I want to say to the gentleman from New York (Mr. Celler) that when they dig into those race riots in Detroit and elsewhere, they will find that the same element promoted them, and they will find the same element stirring up race trouble here in Washington.

When those communistic Jews—of whom the decent Jews are

ashamed—go around here and hug and kiss these Negroes, dance with them, intermarry with them, and try to force their way into white restaurants, white hotels and white picture shows, they are not deceiving any red-blooded American, and, above all, they are not deceiving the men in our armed forces—as to who is at the bottom of all this race trouble.

The better element of the Jews, and especially the old line American Jews throughout the South and West, are not only ashamed of, but they are alarmed at, the activities of these communistic Jews who are stirring this trouble up.

They have caused the deaths of many good Negroes who never would have got into trouble if they had been left alone, as well as the deaths of many good white people, including many innocent, unprotected white girls, who have been raped and murdered by vicious Negroes, who have been encouraged by these alien-minded Communists to commit such crimes.

They are spreading their poisonous doctrine of hate among the Negroes and thereby making it impossible for them to live in peace with the white people around them.

Communism is dying in Russia, or rather it is being run out of Russia by the Russians themselves, but it is still active in this country, as the records of these race riots show.

[Leaflet, Young Communist League of Ypsilanti.]

THERE WAS NO RACE RIOT IN DETROIT—

The riots in Detroit were organized attacks by the Ku Klux Klan and other Fifth Column elements on the Negro people and the war effort.

Hitler boasted that America could be defeated from within by playing on the racial antagonisms. Despite the whitewash by the Governor's committee, there is glaring evidence of the organized character of the disturbance.

The riots are an integral part of an overall plan to disrupt National Unity and create an economic chaos to prevent an immediate European Invasion. It is not a coincidence that similar occurrences have taken place out on the Coast, in Beaumont, Texas; together with the Anti-Negro strikes at Mobile, Alabama; Chester, Pennsylvania; and the recent Packard Strike in Detroit: THEY WERE PLANNED!

A large percentage of the rioters were young people who became the tools of these Fifth Columnists. They did not realize that they were being unpatriotic when they gave way to their racial prejudices and participated in the Detroit insurrection. The War Production

Board in a statement revealed that more man hours were lost in this recent outburst since Pearl Harbor than all the subversive thrusts at the war effort put together!

It is the solemn duty of every patriotic American, Negro and White, to do everything to prevent a re-occurrence.

Workers of Ypsilanti, Negro and White, must unite to their ranks against provocators who may filter in and attempt to foment unrest.

If anyone attempts to inflame your racial prejudice, report them immediately and demand that they be arrested.

Negro people should resist any attempt to provoke them to violence. White people should not become provoked into attack. It is a military necessity that we squelch all efforts aimed at disunity. It is a military necessity that production must not be decreased with strikes against the "Win The War" efforts of Labor and the spreading and displaying of Racial antagonisms.

Citizens! Workers! Let us remain a United Home Front thwarting all attempts to promote disunity. Forward to the Second Front!

[W. K. Kelsey, "The Commentator," *Detroit News*, June 23, 1943.]

What nonsense is this about the racial trouble in Detroit being fifth column activity? Is someone trying to take a slap at the FBI? Is there any evidence whatsoever that a pro-Axis fifth column is operating here? If there is, let's have it. Nothing would be easier to deal with than a fifth column. Bring in the leaders, put 'em out of circulation.

The situation is not that simple. The antagonism between white and black is deep-rooted, and nothing can wipe it out but education —book-education, and education in tolerance. The schools and the churches must deal with it, the press helping.

[From "Factual Report," Rushton, *et al.*, 1943.]

In studying the factors which created that state of mind which made whites and Negroes willing participants in a tragic riot, an answer has been sought to the questions: What particular factor is responsible for the uncontrolled belligerency prevalent in certain white and Negro groups in Detroit? Where have these young hoodlums been told they have a license to lawlessness in their "struggle to secure racial equality?" Who has told them it is proper themselves to redress actual and presumed grievances? Who has exhorted them violently to overthrow established social order to obtain "racial equality"? Who exaggerates and parades before these same elements sordid stories of sensational crime, giving an anti-social complexion to these incidents readily absorbed by the audience? Who constantly beats the drums of: "racial prejudice, inequality, intolerance, discrimination" and challenges these hoodlum elements "militantly" to rise against this alleged oppression? Who charges by their news stories and their editorials that all law enforcement agencies are anti-Negro, brutal, and vicious in the handling of Negroes, and bent upon their persecution? [The Negro press, of course.]

[Among the findings of "Factual Report," Rushton *et al.*, 1943.]

Based upon the statements herein contained, and the indexes here attached, this committee finds:
1. The riot was not planned or premeditated.
2. The riot was not inspired by subversive enemy influence.

What Will Become of Us?

Finally, out of the shattering traumas come warnings that riots threaten the very existence of society. [From William English Walling, "The Race War in the North," *The Independent,* September 3, 1908.]

Either the spirit of the abolitionists, of Lincoln and of Lovejoy must be revived and we must come to treat the negro on a plane of absolute political and social equality, or Vardaman and Tillman will soon have transferred the race war to the North.

Already Vardaman boasts "that such sad experiences as Springfield is undergoing will doubtless cause the people of the North to look with more toleration upon the methods employed by the Southern people."

The day these methods become general in the North every hope of political democracy will be dead, other weaker races and classes will be persecuted in the North as in the South, public education will undergo an eclipse, and American civilization will await either a rapid degeneration or another profounder and more revolutionary civil war, which shall obliterate not only the remains of slavery but all the other obstacles to a free democratic evolution that have grown up in its wake.

[Editorial, *Dallas Morning News,* April 6, 1968.]

If we are candid with ourselves, we must admit that we as a nation began to go astray when we began to accept the notion that laws are less binding upon one man than another. When we began to excuse those whose offenses against law were undertaken in the name of a cause, we undercut that which enables us to live together in peace, our system of laws.

If we search our minds, as well as our hearts, we can see a clear need for restoring respect for laws at the same time that we earnestly seek to change them for the better. If we do not, if we continue to consent to the use of illegal means by those who speak of noble goals, we will certainly see those means destroy not only our goals but our souls.